P9-CLN-517

"Seeing a woman shine in the productivity niche is so refreshing! *On Purpose* is not about goal setting—it is about discovering your passion and purpose so you can achieve the success and meaning *you* deserve. And through her vulnerability and transparency, Tanya draws you in and makes you feel like you can totally do it."

—Allie Casazza, author of *Declutter Like a Mother*

"This is unlike any other personal development or goal setting book out there. *On Purpose* will prove to you that goals are not the goal. Instead, Tanya leads the way—with her signature honesty and boldness—helping you to live each day with intention and guiding you through the steps to a life that feels fulfilling to *you*. This is both the permission slip and the blueprint we all need to stop chasing perfection, discover our individual true purpose, and start living the life we were truly designed to live—one with both success and meaning. I will forever be thankful to Tanya for writing this book!"

—Mary Marantz, bestselling author of *Dirt* and
host of *The Mary Marantz Show*

"This book is the permission slip I didn't know I needed! *On Purpose* allows you to stop chasing perfection and start living the life you desire. Do yourself a favor and devour this book like I did!"

—Jess Ekstrom, author of *Chasing the Bright Side*

"*On Purpose* is a must-read for anyone seeking to find success on their own terms. Tanya Dalton gives you the easy-to-follow actionable guide you've been searching for to take ownership of your life, make intentional choices, and fill your soul with what matters most to you."

—Lisa Hufford, author of *Work Your Way* and
CEO of Simplicity Consulting

ON
PURPOSE

ON PURPOSE

The Busy Woman's Guide to an Extraordinary Life of Meaning and Success

TANYA DALTON

NELSON BOOKS

An Imprint of Thomas Nelson

On Purpose

© 2021 by Tanya Dalton

Published in Nashville, Tennessee, by Nelson Books, an imprint of Thomas Nelson. Nelson Books and Thomas Nelson are registered trademarks of HarperCollins Christian Publishing, Inc.

Published in association with Yates & Yates, www.yates2.com.

Thomas Nelson titles may be purchased in bulk for educational, business, fundraising, or sales promotional use. For information, please email SpecialMarkets@ThomasNelson.com.

Any internet addresses, phone numbers, or company or product information printed in this book are offered as a resource and are not intended in any way to be or to imply an endorsement by Thomas Nelson, nor does Thomas Nelson vouch for the existence, content, or services of these sites, phone numbers, companies, or products beyond the life of this book.

Library of Congress Cataloging-in-Publication Data

Names: Dalton, Tanya, 1974- author.
Title: On purpose : the busy woman's guide to an extraordinary life of meaning and
    success / Tanya Dalton.
Description: Nashville, Tennessee : Nelson Books, [2021] | Includes bibliographical
    references. | Summary: "Nationally recognized productivity expert and bestselling
    author Tanya Dalton delivers a hard-hitting message that will motivate women to step
    into their purpose, invest in themselves, and boldly make their mark on the world"--
    Provided by publisher.
Identifiers: LCCN 2021008588 (print) | LCCN 2021008589 (ebook) | ISBN
    9781400214365 (hardcover) | ISBN 9781400214396 (epub)
Subjects: LCSH: Success. | Self-realization in women.
Classification: LCC BF637.S8 D293 2021 (print) | LCC BF637.S8 (ebook) | DDC
    158.1--dc23
LC record available at https://lccn.loc.gov/2021008588
LC ebook record available at https://lccn.loc.gov/2021008589

Printed in the United States of America

21 22 23 24 25 LSC 10 9 8 7 6 5 4 3 2 1

Tell me, what is it you plan to do
with your one wild and precious life?
—Mary Oliver

To Erika and Curt:
I am lucky to spend my one wild and precious
life with best friends like you.

Living

ON
PURPOSE

isn't about changing who you are;
it's *rising up* and becoming the
best version of you.

CONTENTS

PART THREE: ACTION

PART FOUR: ALTERATION

A NOTE TO THE READER

Dear Reader,

Before we begin, I want you to understand that this book isn't written to help you fit in with the status quo. It's not designed to line up nice and neatly with how society already works. The shelves at your local bookstore are already buckling under the weight of all those other books that tell you what to think, how to behave, and give you rules for getting things done.

This book is none of that.

I want to challenge you to think for yourself. I don't want to tell you *what* to think; I want to empower you to choose *how you want to think*. I want to shake the foundations of how you view your world. Because it is *your* world, and it's filled with opportunities and choices that perhaps you didn't realize were there. Or, more often than not, you've forgotten the choices were there at all.

In the chaotic rush of our days, we can easily get caught up in the "doing" of life, and we sometimes don't take time to pause, step back, and choose. That's what this book is designed to do. It's an intentional pause in your hectic schedule, a chance to take a good look at how you've been going through your days and question how you feel.

We don't talk about our feelings much, do we? Especially when it comes to emotions at work or our mood as a collective society. Sure, we can grumble and complain about irritations or frustrations. But the unadulterated pursuit of happiness is treated as something frivolous or silly.

What, then, is the point of our days? If not to find joy, then what?

Sit and think for a moment about any goal, any dream, you've had in the past. At its heart, wasn't it steeped in happiness?

You wanted a promotion at work. Why?
To feel the satisfaction of climbing the ladder.

You wanted to run a 5K. Why?
To feel the joy of stepping over that finish line.

You wanted to get out of debt. Why?
To feel the happiness of not worrying about paying the bills.

We are operating within dated, obsolete models that are desperately in need of evolving, because joy and happiness deserve to have a seat at the table—it's time to pull up a chair for them. It's not enough to just show up and do our work anymore. We have more time on our hands than ever before in history, so why do we feel rushed and stressed and have an overall dull ache of dissatisfaction?

I want to challenge the bedrock beliefs that so many in our world have wholeheartedly trusted because we were told they were truths. I want to help you have a healthy disregard for the impossible; I want you to see yourself for what you are—a changemaker.

I wrote this book for women who are ready to defy the status quo and stand up and see themselves outside of the tidy definitions society has made for us.

It's time to stop operating at ordinary levels and choose to be extraordinary.

Tanya

HOW THIS BOOK WORKS

There are four sections to this book, with each one designed to build off the last. So while it may be tempting to jump around to the chapters that pull to you, I want to encourage you to read the sections in order. You are, of course, free to go rogue, but allow me to give you a quick overview of the four sections so you can understand how each one connects with the one before it:

REFLECTION: We all have a past. Whether we like that past or not doesn't matter. We can allow it to continue its reign of control or we can use the process of reflection to redefine ourselves as we move toward our future.
- Reflection helps answer the question of *why*: Why do we make the choices we do?

PROJECTION: Using what we learned from Reflection, we will start looking forward—choosing our future. This is the part of the process when many people can feel stuck or uncertain, so together we will unpack ways to clarify what *you* want for your future.
- Projection helps answer the question of *what*: What are the choices we want to make?

ACTION: Once we've projected into our future and explored the possibilities, we want to make sure our actions are aligned with who we have discovered we are and where we want to go. This is an opportunity to release the fears and doubts that keep you from the life you want.

- Action answers the question of *how*: How do we move forward on the choices we're making?

ALTERATION: When we make our plans flexible and we allow for life to happen, we don't get thrown off track when life throws us a curve in the road. In this section we'll find that alteration is sometimes an opportunity for something even better than we dreamed.

- Alteration answers the question of *what if*: What if I get off track?

Here's a truth you'll find inked into these pages: when you choose to expand your possibilities, there's no going back to the old hustle. You will see how you can reignite your passion and excitement for life and let go of burnout because you know how to implement strategies to make life feel easier.

In each of the nine chapters, we cover one choice you are able to make that has the ability to dramatically transform your life for the better. Those nine choices are your foundation to take you from a place of simply dreaming up a better future to a place where you truly feel confident and fully prepared to infuse more and more action into those dreams and goals you set for yourself.

All of the things you envision, all of the success you want, can take flight. There's no need to feel like you are staying stagnant and falling short every time you try to push off the ground. You absolutely have the potential to live *On Purpose*—it's about stepping up and choosing to run your life instead of feeling like life is running you.

You'll find that I write in a raw, unique style. I want you to feel as though I am sitting across from you coaching you through every choice. I include very candid stories about my own journey to help you see how I've navigated through this process in my own life. You'll find I've included stories from women I have worked directly with through my programs and community along with women leaders I admire and respect.

All of these women are very open and honest about their struggles and their triumphs. Most of them have opted to be identified fully in the book, while others found sharing their stories more difficult. For those who preferred anonymity, I've referred to them by a fictitious first name only. But please know that all these women I've included in the book insisted that they wanted their stories told; they believe, as I do, that when we share our journey we light the way for others—especially when that path has been challenging. It is an honor to be able to share these stories with you.

At the end of each chapter I've included many of the common lies we tell ourselves, along with the truths that we've discovered together in the pages before. I also include springboard ideas to help you gain some momentum on your journey because I want to see you succeed.

INTERACTIVE READER'S GUIDE

Like my first book, *The Joy of Missing Out*, we will cover a lot of unique exercises and tactics. To help you dive deeper into these concepts we discuss, I've created a free Interactive Reader's Guide that you can grab at TanyaDalton.com, under the Resources section. You'll find additional stories, thought-provoking activities, and more included with this free resource, designed to make it even easier to bring these concepts into your own life. Go grab that now. I promise you're going to want it.

INTRODUCTION

Your lab results are clear.

I felt a little bit like the wind had been knocked out of me; I even waved my hand behind me, blindly looking for a chair to sink into.* I needed to sit down and take in the weight of that disappointing phrase. Five words that for most people would cue a feeling that might sound like air horns and confetti flittering from the ceiling inside them.

"Are you sure? Did you run my thyroid? What about my hormones?"

I could hear the cloying desperation in my own voice as if I were demanding that they find something—anything—wrong with me. I couldn't see the nurse on the other end of the phone, but I could tell she was shaking her head as she sighed and reminded me, "We ran a full panel. There's absolutely nothing wrong." She paused and then casually added, "You might want to look at your lifestyle."

My lifestyle?!

No.

Just no.

I didn't want to look at my lifestyle—I didn't have time for that. What I needed was a quick solution, a pill or a product I could take to

---

* Admittedly, I've always been prone to being slightly melodramatic.

fix everything. I was tired of being tired. I was frustrated with the extra pounds I was lugging around that made me feel sluggish. And I wasn't the only one who had *had it up to here* with my moods.

I hung up the phone and headed into the kitchen to pour myself a nice, big glass of wine. Apparently there was nothing I could do anyway.

ARE YOU UNCOMFORTABLE ENOUGH?

My friend Tracy once told me, "We don't leave our suffering because it makes us uncomfortable."

It was a funny statement; after all, when we are suffering, don't we want it to end? It's like avoiding the dentist when you have a painful toothache simply because you don't want to hear that you need a root canal.

No one wants a root canal.

What's ironic is the root canal isn't what's painful; it's all the moments leading up to it. Getting the procedure done is actually an opportunity for immediate relief from the pain—not a Band-Aid–type fix but a chance to remove it permanently. There's some discomfort in getting it done, but aren't you already uncomfortable?

It's funny, but, I know for me, the discomfort of suffering didn't seem to outweigh the discomfort of change. Honestly, if I could've picked between taking a good, hard look at my lifestyle or walking barefoot on a bed of hot coals, I probably would have started taking off my shoes.

For the next two months after my phone call, irritation and moodiness became my own runway of hot coals. I slipped into becoming comfortable in my own discomfort. I justified it in every way possible, but late at night, when the house was still and there were no distractions, I couldn't escape my own thoughts. I lay bleary-eyed and wide awake, watching the red numbers of the clock tick by the midnight hours.

I stared at the ceiling and chatted with my regular nighttime visitors: Worry would sit and visit perched on the edge of my bed, while Regret whispered quietly in my ear and Stress hogged all the covers while chattering on at full volume. I couldn't quiet them down. Counting sheep didn't help; neither did counting down the hours: *If I go to sleep now, I'll still get 4 hours of sleep . . . Okay . . . if I fall asleep now, I can still get 3 hours . . . Maybe I can get 2 hours of sleep . . .*

Why did I think it was easier to sit in my suffering? I honestly don't know. I think it's because I felt like this was just the way life was supposed to be.

WHAT ARE YOU FILLING?

I thought I was checking the boxes of everything I was supposed to do. Maybe you feel the same—punching the clock, wrestling your days like an angry bear, dragging yourself through the daily motions, struggling to find satisfaction.

We are filling our calendar, but are we filling our souls?

Have we stopped to ask that question? Or have we resigned ourselves to the belief that this is just how life works? We've been sold a life promise that isn't really true—that if we hustle and suffer through, life will magically work out in the end. Maybe we thought our life map was supposed to look something like this:

GRADUATE
HIGH SCHOOL

ATTEND
COLLEGE

GET A
DEGREE

FIND A
REAL
JOB

GET MARRIED
AND HAVE KIDS

RETIRE

START
ENJOYING LIFE

And when it doesn't, or if we veer off from the "expected" track, we are somehow failing. After all, we live in a world where expectations and perseverance are both put on pedestals, so we get stuck cycling through the soul-crushing motions, living life on repeat, until the day comes that we can retire at the age of 65 . . . *then* we can finally enjoy life a bit.

Stop *borrowing* from

TODAY

to make *tomorrow*

GREAT.

The days of the cushy retirement package are over, and, truth be told, the cheesy gold watch isn't all it's cracked up to be.

And let's be honest, that's not how life really works. We don't have to settle or slog through our days to earn happiness. We have to stop borrowing from today to make tomorrow great. It's time to start living our lives for today *and* for tomorrow. It's time to get a bigger vision—it's time to rise above the mediocrity.

You dream of more? *Go get it.*
You believe you were designed to change the world? *Yes, you were.*
You wonder if you can reach the brass ring? *It's yours to grab.*

It's time to take up more space, to stand tall in the belief of yourself. This is your chance to say: life can be different—life can be *On Purpose.*

LIVING ON PURPOSE

Don't let the word *purpose* fool you—it's such a heavily weighted word. *Purpose* simply means working on something bigger than today—living a life aligned with a larger idea created and set by you. We all have a purpose in our lives, even if we don't know right now what that purpose is. I want you to hear this: you were designed for more. You were made for a life that brings joy and satisfaction to yourself and to others.

We can live each day *On Purpose* by deciding how we want to spend the precious time we have—not waiting for an imaginary clock to wind down so we can one day enjoy life. We have lied to ourselves for far too long. We say it's not possible or we find imaginary obstacles conveniently placed in our path. We make excuses to ourselves because we aren't sure what is truly possible.

I know, because that's exactly what I was doing when I was on the phone begging for a diagnosis from the nurse. I was looking for a magic pill when it really just came down to owning the choices I was making—chasing after success and not taking care of myself because I was too busy trying to look like I had it all together.

Don't feel bad if you've found yourself in a similar situation. Feeling guilt or shame will only hold you back. This is the perfect chance to rise up because of the truth I learned from that hard season:

Once you accept responsibility for your own life, you can do anything.

It doesn't matter what you've done in the past; what matters is what you do moving forward. By picking up this book, you've made the first step in taking back responsibility and deciding how you want to live.

I do think, though, that if we are going to go through this journey together, it's important to clear the air about one thing: this is not just a goal-setting book. Yes, we will talk about goals and how they fit into the big vision you have for your life, but goals are simply the vehicle to get you where you want to go—they are not the end destination.

It's funny because when I sat down to write, I had planned to write an entire book focused solely on goals. I promised my editor, Jenny, that I would write a goal-setting book. I've taught thousands of women how to achieve their goals, so it was easy to give her an outline of each chapter. I could coast into writing two-hundred-some-odd pages only about goal setting.

No problem.

When you decide to write a book, you have to believe you know the topic inside and out. But then you have to step back, give the book room to breathe, and allow it to show you how it needs to unfold. I started with a strict outline, but from the very beginning my writing began to lead me far off the well-beaten path I had planned.

Without question, writing this book has transformed me—as a woman, a business owner, and a mother. It's changed my thinking in ways I never anticipated and shifted the way I run my life at home and in my business. It's infused more joy and harmony into every single day—even on the days where nothing goes as planned.

While I pecked away at my keyboard, the world outside my windows had transformed too. Huge shifts have been happening since the global pandemic. With so many lives upended, the pandemic has acted as a catalyst for many people, causing them to stop and really question whether they've been living their lives *On Purpose*. Asking themselves:

> *I'm exhausted but feel like I've accomplished nothing—what have I been doing with my days?*
> *Why do I feel so unsatisfied with how I'm spending my time?*
> *How do I figure out what to do so my life feels more meaningful?*

Late at night, staring up at the blank white ceiling, those were the same questions I had been asking myself.

BUT WHAT'S THE GOAL?

It had been easy to think that I would write about goal setting; after all, people love goal-setting books. We've convinced ourselves that goals are the magic solution. If we can just accomplish *this one big thing*, suddenly life will be easier. We fixate on the finish line, hoping that maybe happiness will lie in wait on the other side—and are disappointed when it's not.

Sometimes what we think we want is not what we actually need—*goals are not the goal*. When we are so busy focusing on crossing that imaginary finish line, we miss enjoying all the meaningful moments as we make progress. There is an abundance of joy that can be found in the cracks and crevices of our daily life, in the small moments, when we live *On Purpose*.

But because we think goals are the magic solution, we place an incredible amount of importance on the giant achievements, and we discount the small moments. When, in truth, our daily actions will bring us more ongoing joy than a finish line ever will.

In fact, most people undervalue the small, continuous steps because they think that the fastest route between where they are today and the life they dream of is to hustle and constantly chase every opportunity—especially the big, defining ones. The idea of living a life of unhurried purpose feels like it would take too long. The term *unhurried purpose* is a misnomer. It's deceptive because living with unhurried purpose is actually the faster way to get where you want to go. There are no real shortcuts to getting to the ideal life; it simply takes consistent, small movements done with purpose.

That is the heart of this book—the daily choices we make, the small decisions and opportunities that get us to that bigger life we dream about.

We look across the chasm between where we are today versus where we dream of being, and that void is as wide as the Grand Canyon. We fool ourselves into believing that the quickest and easiest way across is to build a jet pack to quickly propel us to the other side. We'll spend 30 years slogging and toiling to create that "faster" way to zoom across the divide in an anticipated 20 seconds flat. We like the idea of that speed.

In reality, simply placing one foot in front of the other on a purposeful path—climbing down into the canyon and then up the rocky trail—would get us where we want to be in just a matter of days—all the while enjoying the views.

Together we will uncover how you can find a more meaningful life in those small, easy steps. We don't realize it, but unhurried purpose is hidden in our daily lives in the choices we make to live our life to the fullest, staying true to the path we believe our soul is designed for.

Living *On Purpose* isn't about changing who you are; it's about rising up and becoming the best version of you. You don't need changing, but there's a good chance your mindset needs a little adjusting. Any time we are ready to uplevel, whether it's in business or our personal life, we need to step out of our comfort zone and question our thinking.

I know I've thought several times that it would be nice to have a crystal ball to show me what the future holds. In truth, there actually is one—if you want to see the clear path of where your life is heading, take a good look at the daily choices you are making.

CHOOSING TO CHOOSE

We have more choices than we think. We just need to open our minds a bit. We aren't talking Jedi mind tricks here—our brain is hardwired to make choices and decisions without skipping a beat.

In fact, we can easily plant a tiny seed of an idea and it immediately begins to grow. This seems like a lot of work, but really it's not. Take yawns, for example. Yawns are one of those things that seem to be contagious. When you see someone else open and stretch their mouth into a satisfying yawn, making a loud *yaaahhhn*, you often feel pulled to yawn yourself. Even reading the word *yawn* in this book right now has you thinking about yawning, doesn't it? I know because as I type the word *yawn* in this passage, I can feel a yawn begging to be released in my own throat.

And with this newfound need to yawn I notice a second, very quiet thought begin to form:

Maybe I'm tired.

Just like that a new thought has been planted. It doesn't matter that all the evidence points the other way. After all, I had a full night's sleep last night and it's 10 a.m. I'm sitting on my screened porch with sunlight pouring onto my lap. I've been up and moving for hours, but I suddenly have the slightest dip in my energy simply because I have decided I am tired.

I'm not really tired, but my brain is tricking me into believing *maybe* I am. That is how powerful our brain is. When it makes a choice—even without our knowledge—we buy in completely.

What if we decided to actually choose our choices?

I know that's an odd statement, but mull that over for a minute. We assume that a choice is always something we actively choose, but it's not. Those yawns are a perfect example of this. Our brain makes thousands of choices every day, and many of those are made without us thinking about them at all. Our brain chooses to pull our hand away when our finger brushes against the hot stove, to shut our eyes when we sneeze, and even to utter a curse word when we bang our shin against something.* We don't intentionally make those choices; our brain chooses them automatically.

Isn't your brain amazing?

Our brain's automatic decisions are a fabulous benefit because I don't want to think too much about my balance when I jerk my leg upward to stop the pain after stepping barefoot on a Lego (again). But it's also a drawback because it means I can easily slip into autopilot, with my brain making decisions about how I live without my conscious knowledge. Not choosing is a choice we often make. When we don't pause and question our thinking from time to time, we can find that we've been sleepwalking through our days.

It's time to choose to be awake in your own life.

When I made that choice for myself, everything changed. I'll admit, at first I felt like a bear being roused out of a long, deep hibernation, but once I wiped the crust of sleep from my eyes, I began to see clearly. *For the first time.*

I started moving forward with vision—clearly seeing the direction I wanted to take. I learned how to create freedom in my life where I actually decided what life looks like (which meant saying goodbye to guilt, overwhelm, and stress). I could see I could be the architect of my own time and how I spend it. I began to discover how life could be so much easier—I just had to wake up and see that if I wanted more joy, more gratitude, and an abundance of love, then I could choose it.

We only have one thing to do before we start. We have to stand in the belief that choosing the life we desire is possible.

Whisper it to yourself. Say it in the mirror in the morning when you get dressed. Post it next to your computer at your desk. You don't need to know how to make those choices right now; we will get there together through the next nine chapters. Right now you just need to be open to seeing that the choices are there.

The first choice is to turn the page and begin. See you in chapter 1.

---

* Crazy interesting fact: your brain chooses to call out vocally when you hurt yourself because it disrupts the pain messages. But why does it always seem to make you say the curse word louder if your kids are within earshot?

part one

REFLECTION

Answers the Question: Why?

one

CHOOSE TO DISRUPT YOUR PATTERNS

It's just going to be one of those days.

We've all said it. We wake up in the morning and the day seems destined for failure within 30 minutes of opening our eyes.

Maybe you woke up late and are tearing around the bathroom scrambling to get dressed while shouting feverishly down the hall to get everyone else moving.

But no one else seems to feel the urgency to move, making your irritation level rise to DEFCON 2.

Or maybe you stumbled groggily to the kitchen for your morning cup of joe only to be suddenly jarred awake by the white-hot pain of stubbing your toe on the doorframe.

Coffee won't fix that.

Or maybe you are just so ridiculously tired, and the idea of pulling off the warm covers to go to the gym feels like a monumental effort. So you hit snooze just one time . . . okay two . . . maybe three.

And then feel heavy guilt shrouding you all day long for skipping your workout.

Somehow the day is already made, the course has been set, and there's no changing it or veering off the path. It's just going to be one of *those* days.

PATTERNS AND DISRUPTIONS

As humans, we are drawn to patterns. When we see a pattern, we believe there's no breaking it. It's fixed and set in stone. It is what it is. Unfortunately, we can allow this idea of permanence to hold us back. When something negative happens, we hold fast on to it and we hold it up as absolute evidence that this is just how life is destined to be.

What I find so fascinating with our brain is how we steadfastly— almost stubbornly—cling to the negative. Did you know that our brain is actually hardwired to see the negative five times more than it will see (and remember!) a positive experience? Five.

This negativity bias was wired to help us survive—historically we needed to remember the negative in order to live another day and pass our genes down the line. Obviously, this was great for our cave ancestors to help them remember not to touch the fire and to avoid the saber-tooth tiger, but in today's world it means we have a hard time seeing past the negatives.

This happens so often with our past. We look behind us and we see the trail of where we have been and what we have done, and it's littered with bad experiences, decisions we regret, and trauma that feels like it defines us. It's hard to see the strength we gained by overcoming the challenges, the lessons we learned when we picked ourselves up after failing. All we can see is a pattern of mistakes and failures.

This is one of the reasons that the idea of looking back and reflecting can feel like something we'd prefer to avoid. We want to shove it under the bed—the same way I dealt with my dirty laundry when I was told to clean my room at age thirteen. It was there . . . and the room wasn't really clean. That pile of dirty laundry was subtly adding a lingering odor of mildew. I knew it, and anyone who walked into my room knew it.

YOUR BRAIN AT 88 MPH

We show up every day with our baggage—our pile of dirty laundry. But we are so used to having it around, we don't even notice the smell. We've gone noseblind, but it's there . . . adding its aroma to anything and everything we do. We allow the disappointments in our past to obscure our view of the future. We see a pattern and we believe we're stuck—and the rut is so deep we cannot see out.

Our brain, though, loves patterns. It likes being able to guess the ending based on what it already knows. So when the pattern doesn't really work, it confuses us. It's why we are gobsmacked when Jo somehow doesn't end up marrying Laurie in *Little Women*. Or why we gasped out loud the first time we heard Darth Vader utter the words "I am your father" to Luke. It doesn't fit.* How is it possible?!

But not all patterns are designed to continually repeat until the end of time. Many need to be broken. Yes, patterns create order—and no matter who you are (I'm looking at you, Enneagram 7s), your mind likes a nice foundation of order. It relies on order to make assumptions about what will happen next. That's what our brain does. It creates order out of chaos so we can move through our daily lives.

Can you imagine how taxing it would be if we didn't rely on patterns? If everything in our world was a surprise? It would be exhausting if we were perpetually excited and distracted about every tiny thing—the spray of water shooting from the spigot when we turn on the shower or the way the sun filters through the slats of the blinds.

Michael Pollan explained it like this: our brain uses what it learned in the past to "develop shorthand ways of slotting and processing our every experience." We want to know what to expect next, so "our brains [are] continually translating the data of the present into the terms of the past,

---

* Interesting fact: During shooting, Star Wars creator George Lucas intentionally replaced that line with "Obi Wan killed your father." He knew that the real line would be a shock to audiences, so he intentionally kept it a secret. Only three people knew the true line of dialogue before the premiere, when fans were stunned at the revelation.

reaching back in time for the relevant experience, and then using that to make its best guess as to how to predict and navigate the future."

In other words, our brain uses its own Marty McFly time machine to constantly hop back in time to see what's happened in our past so it can guess what will happen in the future. Creating order.

It does this with mind-numbing speed—we don't even realize we are doing this. Yes, mind numbing, because it dulls the hope of possibility: *What if this time* is *different from the last?*

Thanks to our brain's love of patterns, we can get hung up on our past mistakes and failures to the point where we make ourselves afraid of what could possibly happen next. Our brain takes over and insists on filling in the gaps, making guesses about our future. It plugs them in the spaces like autocorrect on your computer. Yes, it's helpful . . . but then there are the times you hit Send too fast on your text or email only to realize your message is utterly and entirely wrong. We've all done that—shot off a quick message and then scrambled to fix it.

What if your brain is sometimes wrong? What if the most "logical answer" isn't the right one?*

Because here's the truth: the thing our brain forgets is that all the trials we've gone through up to this moment are the very things that have helped shape us into the people we are today and the people we are striving to become tomorrow. We just have to learn how to break the patterns.

Every failure, every experience—the good and the bad—has, in one way or another, led us to this exact moment.

These are the treasures hidden in our minds, nestled in that pile under our beds among the dirty laundry. Those things that, in the moment, felt like they were happening to you, but with the beauty of hindsight, you can now see that those things were really happening *for* you—to help you become who you are right this very second. I know that sounds like

---

* Please note: The term *logical answer* must be said in a Spock voice. If you just read that line and didn't hear Spock speaking in your head, please go back and reread it.

it should be written on a Hallmark card—and maybe it should, because it's true.

But you cannot find the treasures among the trash unless you pull all of that junk out. Spread it on the floor and take a good, hard look at it. Dig and start mining for the gold that's hiding underneath the piles.

LOOK BACKWARD TO MOVE FORWARD

If you want to move forward, you have to begin by looking back. It may seem counterintuitive, but looking behind helps illuminate the path ahead. Reflection is such a key element to discovering who you really are and who you want to become. I call them breadcrumbs—the little things that have marked the path of where you've been. Breadcrumbs are incredibly helpful in unlocking who you are at your core. And they can help reveal how and where to invest in yourself.

Reflection is an incredibly powerful exercise, but it's something we instinctively want to avoid. I know you don't want to dive into your past. I know you can come up with about 5 million other things you can do to avoid looking back—including deep cleaning your cat's litter box or starting that new vegan cleanse you've been talking about doing for the past 6 months. Here's a question I want you to think about as we talk about this idea of reflection:

Would you rather stay stuck living in the past, in a life that no longer exists?
or
Would you rather celebrate the many things you've already been through—the good and the bad—so you can start to live your future?

Taking time to reflect requires having the courage to acknowledge that your life has included negative experiences. Having hardship or failure in our lives doesn't make any one of us unique. Learning how to deal with the negative is a skill we all need to sharpen because life is always going to be filled with incredible highs and, yes, some occasional deep lows.

Of course, when we are digging into that laundry pile, we will—and should—look for the positive. The good pieces of our past can help us see what we're capable of accomplishing; they give us springboards to know what we do well and what we can build upon to bring us successes. The shiny, happy moments are fun to look at—like little trophies lined up in a glass case. Pieces of plastic spray-painted gold and shellacked until they shine, they stand up as proof that we've done good. Let me correct that . . . we believe they stand up as proof that *we are good*. It's easy to want to pull them out of the case and proudly hold them above our heads like Rocky at the top of those steps.

To be honest, though, the hardships, the failures, the mistakes, the trauma—those are the most fertile ground of all. That's where we can plant our seeds for learning who we want to become in moving forward. Knowing what we like is helpful, but knowing what we don't like, what we don't want to repeat, is more than helpful—it's powerful.

It's easy, though, to miss the gift because of the package it's wrapped in. We are so caught up in the disappointment, in the thick, oozy hurt, that we cannot see the pain as part of the process. Hidden inside is a tiny flicker of what it is we truly want in our lives.

Did you know that people are inherently more likely to take action to move away from pain than they are to move toward pleasure? What that means is pain and hardship are a stronger motivator than the good. This is why we need to mine for those tough parts of the past. When we hold them up to light, we can clearly see exactly what it is that we want to avoid, which means it also shows us what we truly want.

Think about it. We don't necessarily get motivated to get up and exercise until maybe our pants get a little tight. *Oof.* We don't stop working long hours until we realize we've missed dinner with the family. Again.

Pain, frustration, and negative feelings are God's own way of signaling to us to stop and take note of what is being birthed inside of us.

It's easy to *miss* the

GIFT

because of the
package it's
wrapped in.

PURPOSE IN THE PAIN

I gained so much insight into my own past when reading Harold Kushner's book *When Bad Things Happen to Good People*. Reading his thoughts on pain helped me see how purpose is often buried within the pain of my own life. I want to share his words with you, in hopes that it does the same:

> [Scientists] have determined that two of the most painful things human beings can experience are giving birth and passing a kidney stone. From a purely physical point of view, these two events both hurt equally, and hardly anything hurts more. But from a human point of view, the two are so different.
>
> The pain of passing a kidney stone is simply pointless suffering, the result of a natural malfunction somewhere in your body. But the pain of giving birth is creative pain. It is pain that has meaning, pain that gives life, that leads to something.
>
> This is why the person who passes a kidney stone will usually say "I'd give anything not to have to go through that again," but the woman who has given birth to a child . . . can transcend her pain and contemplate repeating the experience. Pain is the price we pay for being alive.

I know it may be hard to understand why the pain is there, still raw and tender. Let me be frank—no matter what you think you might have done to earn that hurt, you didn't. I didn't deserve it; you didn't deserve it. None of us do. But "pain is the price we pay for being alive."

I'm not saying we need to be grateful for these difficult parts of our past, but we can appreciate what they show us. One of the most courageous things we can do is choose to pick ourselves back up and realize that season we lived through—the hardship, the tragedy, the place where we felt stuck—is "creative pain."

All that we live through—the good, the bad, and the really bad—all of it allows us to have perspective. Changing our perspective on pain is difficult to do, but when we see that these experiences are all part of our journey to get us where we are meant to be, it can make moving through them easier.* It's the stumbling blocks of today that lead us to the springboards of tomorrow.

Knowing what you don't want clearly reveals what you *do*. Start by looking at the painful parts of your past—the things you regret or have remorse for not doing, the places where shame blooms and grows, the parts of your past you don't want to repeat. Only when you acknowledge that they exist can you actively make choices to disrupt those patterns and make strides in the direction you really want to move.

DISRUPTING A PATTERN IN JUST FIVE WORDS

Myoshia Boykin-Anderson has a past that is filled with hardship and trauma that could have dragged her down and kept her from her true potential. Raised in the inner-city Third Ward of Houston by a drug-addicted mom, she finds herself pregnant not long after graduation. She's smart and loves science and math, but when the time comes to consider college, she knows she cannot leave her siblings behind. She has a passion for technology, but with no degree, life is a struggle filled with temp jobs and living paycheck-to-paycheck.

We already know where this story is going. Our brain sees the patterns—these markers—and the path for this woman is clear. We see a girl who could have had potential, but the deck is stacked high against her. There's no choice for her to make—it's all out of her control.

Maybe it feels like no surprise to learn that Myoshia finds herself on a cold February morning sitting in her manager's office learning that the technical company she has been working for is shutting its doors, effective immediately. And, just like that, she finds herself with no job, no savings, and a hungry daughter to feed.

---

* *Easier* is a relative term here; I don't want to pretend it's going to be simple. Talk to someone—a counselor, a trusted friend, a therapist. Don't undervalue the importance of seeking support and help from others.

Fits the pattern, doesn't it?

I can imagine the scene—maybe you can too. A young mom sitting nervously erect across from a large desk with her eyes slightly wider than normal, taking it all in, hearing the words *You no longer have a job* rushing into her ears. Myoshia told me that as she sat in that woman's office absorbing those words, she made a decision.

A small voice in her head said: *This is the last time anyone is going to say that to me.* And with that mighty phrase, the rhythmic pattern of her past skipped. It no longer worked.

It wasn't a magic button—life didn't suddenly come easy—but there was a noticeable shift. Myoshia shared with me, "I didn't know what I would do, but what I did know, was that I didn't want to allow that to happen again. If I could control it, no one else was going to be able to decide whether I could generate income and take care of my family."

Myoshia changed her thinking. Instead of getting caught up in her own hurt of losing a job, she focused on the fact that there were now sixty-three clients with no service provider. That small shift in thinking was like drops of gasoline on a spark inside her.

She helped her manager clean and close the office and then walked out the door, taking her stack of client names with her. She chose to see an opportunity—not an end, but a beginning.

Working her way down the list, she called each of her contacts to see if she could step in as their new provider. Now, if this were a movie, this would be the scene as the closing credits begin to scroll because we would know that, of course, they would need her. Of course they would want her. Of course, this was the first day of the rest of her beautiful life. Of course, of course.

Every single one of them said no.

I'm sure Myoshia felt the crushing weight of disappointment each time she heard that word, but instead of crawling into the corner or letting it be a sign from the universe that it wasn't meant to be, she asked if it would be okay to check back in March.

And that's what she did—every month she would choose a Friday to go through the remaining names on the list and call them again. All of them continued to say no. Month after month, Myoshia called, slapped a smile on her face, listened to their no, and followed it up by asking if she could call again the next month. Nine months later, her list was whittled down to sixteen names, but she chose to pick up the phone anyway and keep asking if someone needed her services.

On the sixth call on a Friday in November, she heard, "As a matter of fact . . ."

"I became an entrepreneur with those five words," Myoshia says now. During her lunch break that day, she ran down to city hall and filed her business. There were times when she felt like she was flying by the seat of her pants. (We all feel like that from time to time, don't we?) There were lots of valleys and more setbacks than you can imagine, but she kept making the choice to move forward.

Her business hit six figures and then seven. Myoshia is now the founder of a successful multimillion-dollar tech company. Her purpose, she says, is to show others that it can be done.

"I believe in *Why not me?* I want other women and young girls to see what's possible. When you look at my story, this was not supposed to be—but it is. And not by happenstance."

Her company is an extension of that. She shows business owners what is possible through technology—and how they can grow their businesses by creating solutions to their own problems. And she models what is possible through her own life. These weave together as her purpose.

Myoshia's actions speak to a truth that is written within all of our stories: There are no closed doors—they're all cracked open a little. You just have to choose to push it open. Or kick it in. Or rip it off its hinges. There are no unbreakable patterns.

Knowing that she didn't want to be jobless again gave her the incentive to look harder for the shiny trophies in her past and build off them—for Myoshia this was the knowledge she had gained in all those different tech jobs over the years. Her wide range of experience gave her an expertise she might not have otherwise recognized.

YOU HAVE MORE CONTROL THAN YOU THINK

We cannot give in and tell ourselves the lie that nothing can be done. We have to stop giving ourselves the excuse that the world is working against us. Do some people have it easier than you? Yes. Someone is always going to have it easier. It's only by the sheer force of choice that you can make that inconsequential.

We can choose to be put down and made to feel small by the things in our lives that we cannot control or we can choose to take ownership over what we can control.

And I understand that the word *control* is a touchy one. I find that a lot of people bristle at it because they don't like the idea of being controlling or being labeled a "control freak." We have a complicated relationship with that word because we worry about what it looks like to others. But understanding what we can control versus what we cannot will build our confidence in extraordinary ways. It allows us to relinquish and release that which we do not control, and it allows us to take full ownership of what we can.

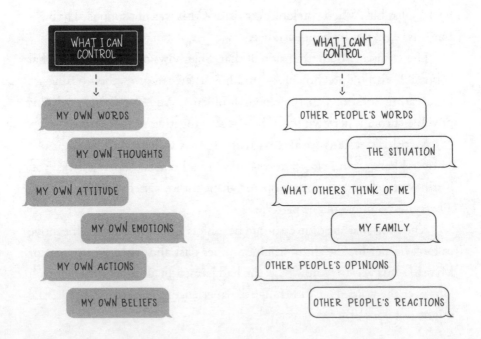

We need to focus on what we can control, including our emotions, desires, judgments, creativity, determination, and, of course, mindsets. This allows us to grow beyond the things we can't control and instead change our attitudes toward them.

So often we fixate on the things in our lives that we cannot control—the forces of nature, the medical diagnosis, the people who have wronged us. That's the big one right there—how other people view us: their reactions and opinions, their choices, judgments, or actions. We cannot control any of these things.*

Yes, there are a million things we *cannot* control, but the things that we can are mighty and strong. We can control our reactions, our behaviors, our efforts, and our choices. We can choose to disrupt old patterns and take ownership of our future. We cannot always control the outside world, but we can control what goes on inside our own heads.

GOOD GRIEF

Meaghan B Murphy is one of the most upbeat, fully-charged women I've ever met. Her high-energy joy is absolutely contagious—when you are in the room with her, you cannot help but want to chase excitement right alongside her.

It's no surprise to me that Meaghan's purpose is tied to spreading positive energy, which she calls "finding your moments of yay." But, shockingly, Meaghan isn't a natural-born optimist. "My nickname as a kid was Grumpy," she confided to me.

When her father was diagnosed with pancreatic cancer and passed away within five months, she knew it would be easy to slip into negativity like a pair of old, comfortable shoes. But she decided she wanted to do something different. "I didn't want to keep talking about . . . the sadness. I just wanted to see the good," she decided.

---

* And cats. We cannot control cats.

Meaghan created an exercise for herself that she dubbed Operation Good Grief. She chose to look for one positive thing every day—just one. In a time when nothing seemed happy, it caused her to dig deep. One good thing can be very hard to find in a season filled with sadness, but Meaghan committed and found at least one little pocket of joy every day. And then it started to snowball. "We have control over our emotions and our happiness. 'Choose Happy' isn't just a bumper sticker, it's actually something you can do," she realized.

"That's why I'm so passionate about [spreading positivity], because I realize that anybody . . . can live like this . . . I retrain[ed] myself to more wholeheartedly and actively find the good because I'm a person who's inherently negative." Meaghan continues to spread and encourage joy in thousands of ways through her books, her social media feed, and her work as editor-in-chief at *Woman's Day*, where she infuses joy into thousands of women's lives through the pages of the magazine.

I don't want to make light of your past. I understand there may be parts of your history that are seeping with pain, but I would challenge you to see also that there are moments of sheer delight and happiness scattered there as well. You cannot have valleys in your life map if you don't also have some peaks.

WHERE'S THE PONY?

Seeing those peaks can be difficult in the moment, but there's a phrase I like to use at times like that: find the pony.

It's not my own saying; it's one I borrowed from former president Ronald Reagan, who used that phrase when living in the White House. Whenever something would go wrong, as it inevitably would, someone on his staff would say, "There must be a pony in here somewhere." In other words, when the world gives you a pile of manure, you start searching around for that pony.

The saying is actually based on a story, hundreds of years old, about a father with two sons—one eternally pessimistic and the other unwaveringly optimistic. The father decides he wants to test the boys, so he places both of them in a room filled with manure.

After an hour, he opens the door to find the pessimistic boy angry and irritated about being stuck in a room filled with manure. The optimist, though, cannot be found. Finally the dad spots him, digging deep into the manure with both hands. Shocked, the father asks him what in the world he is doing. Grinning, the boy looks up and says, "With all this manure there's got to be a pony in here somewhere!"

We can choose to just see the shit or we can choose to start looking for a pony in the pile of life. It's a choice.

Changing your life situation and circumstance sometimes isn't possible, or at least isn't possible in the short term. Sometimes all you can do is change your perspective, belief, or opinion about the situation.

THE FIFTH WHY

Changing your perspective allows you to grow beyond the things you can't control and change your attitude toward them instead. But how do you do this? How do you find that pony when the room seems to be completely filled with manure? I'm going to share with you a method that has worked for me and for women I have coached. It's called the Fifth Why.

It's similar to a technique often used in the field of productivity as a way to discover the root cause of a problem or issue. Business operations manuals call it the "Five Whys." In manufacturing, it's looking for the bottleneck—the stopgap that keeps production from moving forward.

That's what we've got right here—an emotional bottleneck that may be slowing you down from reaching your true potential.

I call this method the Fifth Why for several reasons:

- You are not a factory, so I want us to embrace the fact that this method helps us get to the heart of why we *feel* the way we do. And because we are focused on feelings and not just data, I think it's important to call it something different.
- With this technique, it really is the Fifth Why that holds the key to unlocking the real issue, so let's highlight that. It allows for a deeper dive, but not so deep that we risk getting the bends or losing our way. The Fifth Why is what we want to focus on.
- Honestly? I think the alternative—the Five Whys—is a terrible name. I do. It feels like we asked a toddler to name the method, the same way my sister, Kim, named our new dog *Puppy* when she was in preschool. And, yes, we continued to call the dog Puppy even when she was old and gray twelve years later.

I've used the Fifth Why technique to help people explore gratitude, to find problems in their production systems, to find the root cause of what's holding them back. I've used it in parenting, as a boss and manager and as a business coach. This technique works far beyond the manufacturing floor. This is one of those exercises that is deceptively simple. It's easy to do, but incredibly powerful to discover your root cause.

Let's channel our inner three-year-old—let's ask *Why*. No more simply accepting the status quo, no more excuses about how this is just how life is. If we want to take charge of our lives, we need to get curious and ask why.

Remember when you were in preschool? If you were like most kids, you asked why almost one hundred times a day. By middle school, though, the questioning stopped. We were rewarded for answers—not questions. And so we stopped wondering why—why we feel the way we do or why the sky is blue—and we started just accepting life as it is.

It's time for us to question everything.

Let's dive into the Fifth Why:

Start by defining the problem or issue. What is it you see as a problem? Write it out as a statement:

I feel like a failure.

Then ask yourself why. And then write it out with the reason:

I feel like a failure because I didn't get the promotion at work last month.
  PROBLEM   1ST WHY

Then insert your reason (your first why) into the beginning part of the next sentence and repeat the question *why*:

I didn't get the promotion at work because my boss didn't think I was ready.
        1ST WHY   2ND WHY

Keep repeating the process until you get to the Fifth Why:

My boss didn't think I was ready because I haven't gotten my advanced
        2ND WHY   3RD WHY
certification.

I haven't gotten my advanced certification because I don't have time to
        3RD WHY   4TH WHY
work on it after hours.

I don't have time to work after hours because I am not really planning my
        4TH WHY   5TH WHY
time and the evening seems to just get away from me.

The key is to take your time. Focus on the facts—even the facts you don't like. The reason why may not come to you at first. Give yourself space and grace. Let go of judgment.

I feel like what might be most helpful here is for you to see a real-life example of my own. I went and dug out my old journal and found where I did this for myself after a trauma I experienced. Talk about raw. This is not easy to share, but I think it's important for you to see how the technique helped me. I'm including my notes so you can see how I worked through it.

I feel scared to be alone.

IS THIS TRUE? NO, I'M
SCARED ALL THE TIME.

I feel scared all the time.

I NEED TO CALL IT WHAT IT REALLY IS
INSTEAD OF HIDING BEHIND WORDS THAT
MAKE IT SOUND INSIGNIFICANT.

I feel scared all the time because I worry that ~~it's going to happen again.~~ I'm going to be attacked again.

I worry that I'm going to be attacked again because I really thought I
                    AND SMART
was being careful ^last time.

I thought I was being careful and smart last time because I wasn't drinking.

I wasn't drinking because I wanted to feel more in control of my situation.

I wanted to feel more in control of my situation because I don't trust other people.   THE REAL ISSUE

Let's be honest here. Recognizing that I didn't trust people didn't feel like the pony—it felt like the manure. Like a big smelly pile of manure. But it was the pony because once I realized this was key to me being able to feel safe, I could confront it from a rational place. Emotions are important—all emotions—the good, the bad, and the really ugly. But we need to look at them from outside the rawness, outside the hurt, and bring them to light.

Our lives have highs and lows—but sometimes when we are in a low, it feels so deep we think we'll never climb out. But we will. If you look at the patterns—at the breadcrumbs of your life—you'll see that again and again we do experience highs after the lows. We need both in our lives.

Of course, none of us want the lows. No one gets excited about the deep wells in our life map, but hiding them doesn't make them go away. It only gives them more power. We need to bring them to light. Only when we acknowledge them can we see how that beautiful brokenness has made us who we are.

WHAT YOU CAN'T ALWAYS SEE IS STILL THERE

In the predawn hours of January 17, 1994, the people of the San Fernando Valley region of Los Angeles were jarred awake by the massive tremors of a 6.7 magnitude earthquake. Electrical lines were snapped, buildings crumbled like houses of cards, and highways buckled and split in the shocks that hit the city.

As the rumbling and shaking died away, people rushed outside dazed and stunned. They gazed around them and then gasped as they glanced upward and saw what many of them described as a strange sky with a giant silvery cloud. The phone lines at the police stations and Griffith Observatory rang incessantly with panicked calls from frightened citizens assuming that the eerie sight above was responsible for the destruction around them.

But there were no alien visitors above—it was simply the Milky Way bathing the skies in all her glory. With all the lights extinguished, most of the residents of the City of Angels were getting their first glimpse of the beautiful band of stars and planets—a sight that cannot normally be seen due to the glow of their city.

If you've ever gone to a remote spot in our world and had the privilege of gazing up at a Milky Way sky, you know it's an awe-inspiring sight making you feel infinitesimally small and yet filled with absolute wonder at the same time.

That sky shines above us every single night whether we see it or not—it's only when we allow ourselves to take some time away from the bright lights that we can marvel in the beauty it holds. Our past is no different—there are points of brightness and wonder and there are pockets of ink-black darkness. Both are needed to create the beautiful life we want, and both are there whether or not we choose to look—the magic is there creating a beautiful trail of breadcrumbs behind it. We simply need to take some space to peer back into our pasts to allow us to see ourselves as perfectly imperfect.

LIES THAT HOLD YOU BACK:

- I am powerless; the universe is against me.
- I can't change anything.
- This is just the way things are, I guess.
- I don't want to think about this.

TRUTHS THAT MOVE YOU FORWARD:

- When I look at my past, I can see that I'm stronger than I ever realized.
- When I am honest with myself, I have the ability to change my perspective.
- If I choose to look deeper, things will get better.
- I choose to think about this because growth happens outside of my comfort zone.

SPRINGBOARD: Make sure to download the free Interactive Reader's Guide to help you start the reflection process. Go to TanyaDalton.com/Resources.

two

CHOOSE YOUR IDENTITY

Who are you?

It seems like a simple enough question. After all, you get asked it all the time. But the bigger question is: How do you answer it? Or rather, how do you identify yourself?

Do you define yourself by who you aspire to be, or do you cling to the patterns of your past? We all use titles and labels in a thousand different ways, many times unknowingly concreting those negative patterns for ourselves.

We use words like *smart, lazy, unmotivated, kind, fat, slow*—the list goes on and on. We hide behind our words and labels. We forget we have the ability to choose how we describe ourselves.

Sarah Breedlove understood the power of choosing your own labels and how they single-handedly can shift your patterns into something brand new.

No one would have guessed Sarah was born with a deep purpose that had the potential to change the world. After all, she was born to emancipated slaves and toiled away her childhood on a plantation. She became a wife at fourteen, a mother at seventeen, and a widow at nineteen.

In fact, when the world saw her, they didn't see potential. They saw a tired washerwoman with patchy, balding hair and a hungry daughter clinging to her skirts. Looking back at the years behind her, all anyone could see was a pattern of low self-esteem and backbreaking work. For a long time, that was all Sarah could see too.

But one morning, standing in front of her tub with a load of wash before her, she had a new thought. She later shared, "As I bent over the washboard and looked at my arms buried in soapsuds, I said to myself: 'What are you going to do when you grow old and your back gets stiff? Who is going to take care of your little girl?'"

Sarah knew in that moment that she didn't want to worry about her daughter's future; she knew she didn't want her daughter bent over a hot washtub day after day. Knowing what she didn't want made clear what she did. She wanted a different pattern, and with that thought, her path forked into something new.

If Sarah were to dive into her Fifth Why, I feel certain she would have discovered that her appearance was at the heart of her low self-confidence. In fact, once she discovered a hair remedy that transformed her appearance, she felt her self-esteem transform as well. She knew she wanted to share the confidence-building tonic with other women.

When she married Charles Joseph Walker, she decided she no longer wanted to define herself as a poor washerwoman. She wanted to identify herself as someone grander. She wanted a moniker that reflected her newborn confidence as she began to sell her hair tonic.

Instead of adding on the traditional *Mrs.* to her name, she began referring to herself as *Madam* C. J. Walker. She "wanted to create this larger life image of [herself]," according to her great-great-granddaughter A'Lelia Bundles. She felt it added a sophisticated French flair and hinted that she was more than just a former laundress and cook. In a time when most Black women were addressed by surname only or as *Auntie*, Madam Walker's new moniker was a signal of self-respect. Not only was she breaking the patterns of her past, she was breaking the patterns of society as well.

Madam Walker's purpose was to do more than help women feel beautiful; she wanted them to experience that same strength and confidence she felt.

She was intent on helping empower women of color, and she did that by creating a company that established an entirely new standard for African American beauty. She pioneered using real Black women in her advertising rather than Whites, which was the norm. She became an advocate and an activist for Black women and expanded her business to create change politically and socially. Madam Walker is widely regarded as the first female self-made millionaire and as an agent of change, converting tens of thousands of customers into employees and providing them with opportunities to rise above the poverty level and create an independent life for themselves.

A woman who started life in the backbreaking work of picking cotton rose to historical and social significance by identifying herself as more.

WHO ARE YOU?

Madam Walker went so far as to change her title from Mrs. to Madam. So, again, the question for you is, How do you identify *yourself*?

Simon Sinek shared that "one of the ways we are able to deceive ourselves comes from the words we use . . . [which] allow us to disassociate ourselves from the impact of decisions or actions." The words we choose to describe ourselves start to define us.

After all, what we tell ourselves is what we believe. And what we believe is what we receive. Our beliefs become our reality.

I know—you might be saying to yourself that's some woo-woo stuff right there. I understand it feels touchy-feely, but it's absolutely true. What we believe is what we receive. There are a multitude of studies that prove the life-changing magic of a positive, productive view of yourself and of life as a whole. One of my favorites is known as the Nun Study, which is regarded as one of the most powerful studies of how our attitude impacts us.

Nuns are a fascinating group. You'd be hard-pressed to find another large group of people who live in similar ways: their living situations, their food, their lifestyle and work are all highly regulated because of the vows they have taken. One of the few variables then is attitude and outlook.

What we *tell ourselves* is what we

BELIEVE.

And what we *believe* is what we

RECEIVE.

Our beliefs *become our*

REALITY.

Researchers were given access to the journals and autobiographies of several cloisters of nuns from the 1930s and '40s. The women, at the time of their writings, were about twenty-two years old and just entering their convents. Analysts pored over the words, written almost sixty years earlier, that each woman used to describe her situation and outlook. What they found was astonishing.

Based on the words they chose to use in their writings, nuns were categorized in one of three groups: positive, negative, or neutral. Sisters who used words like *hope, love,* or *gratefulness* garnered a position in the positive group, while words like *shame, fear,* or *disgust* placed those women into the negative category.

When the researchers looked at the women's lifespans, what they found was incredible. An astonishing 54 percent of nuns who had looked at life with a positive view were still alive and thriving at the age of ninety-four, compared to only 15 percent of their more negative sisters. Those women with a positive outlook, on average, lived as much as a full decade longer.

What fascinates me most, though, is that this research wasn't about living longer—it was about Alzheimer's and the effects positivity has on contracting the disease. Again there was an astonishing connection. Those who were most positive seemed to avoid the disease—only fifteen of the positive-thinking nuns were found to have evidence of Alzheimer's in their brains upon their death. But here's the most interesting twist: out of those fifteen women, not one of them outwardly displayed symptoms of dementia.

Our words matter. What I'm hoping and praying you'll see here is that how we describe ourselves and our situations deeply affects us. It's not New Agey stuff—this is science-backed truth.

WORDS OF REDEMPTION OR REPULSION

So when you dove into your past and you pulled all of the dirty laundry out from under your bed, how did you describe it? Or rather, how did you describe *you*?

We all know the fear of being unworthy; we've all felt shame and disappointment. Understanding this connects us, but it does not define us. The opposite of failure is not success—it's redemption, which is even more powerful because it means we have overcome.

So, again, the question goes to you—do you use words of redemption, words of pride and strength to describe yourself? Or do you choose words like *failure*, *lazy*, or *unlucky*?

Your words matter.

Words can act as a balm upon the rough spots or they can act as a stinging curse. When we choose to label ourselves in negative ways, we are forming a strong pattern of bedrock beliefs. We begin to believe we are cursed with continually being a failure, that we are stuck being lazy, or we buy in to the story that we are simply unlucky.

When you have a constant repetition of this diatribe, it channels a deep mental groove in your brain that makes it easy to believe that "This is just the way I am and there's no changing it."

Think about the words or phrases you use to identify yourself right now. Do they sound like any of these?

I'm a terrible public speaker.
Nothing ever goes right for me.
I am the worst with money.
Technology hates me.
I never finish anything.
No one wants to pay me what I'm worth.

If so, it's no surprise you believe them. You've said them to yourself so many times, they've formed grooves in your mind so deep they might as well be the Grand Canyon. These words feel like they define you—and they confine you. They keep you from the greatness you deserve.

You have the power to change the words you use. So often we feel like we are stuck and there's no changing who we are—or where we are going—but we can hike our way out of that Grand Canyon groove. Yes, it's a big hike and it's going to take some sweat equity, but all you need to do is choose to take the first step.

STOP WAITING FOR PERMISSION

A few months ago I was at the Atlanta airport on my way to a speaking event. I was moving from one terminal to the next, lugging my not-so-light carry-on behind me and wrestling unsuccessfully with the heavy shoulder strap on my laptop bag. The woman behind me on the escalator gave an exaggeratedly loud sigh and muttered something under her breath that was definitely passive-aggressive.

I could tell she was irritated, so I turned and faced her. She looked embarrassed and avoided eye contact, but I engaged anyway. I smiled and said, "Airports are a gauntlet, right? If you are in a hurry, I'm happy to move so you can pass."

Still avoiding eye contact, her eyebrows lifted in surprise. "Yes," she muttered. "I'm worried about my flight." I moved aside quickly, wished her good luck, and watched her get swallowed by a sea of passengers as she hustled to her gate.

Here's the thing: *all she had to do was ask.*

That frustration she was feeling? That irritation bubbling up inside her? It was 100 percent avoidable. Relief was there; all she needed to do was ask. But how often do we speak up? We have more control over our situation than we pretend we do—we simply need to make it happen.

I DON'T OR I CAN'T

Taking charge of you and your situation doesn't make you a control freak; it makes you accountable. It makes you the owner of who you are and what you want. Even small words communicate attitude and outlook to your brain. For example, did you know that choosing to use the words "I don't" instead of "I can't" will make you twice as successful when trying to make healthy choices?

It's a small but powerful adjustment. When faced with temptation—like a big, thick slice of chocolate cake with frosting slathered on top—saying, "I *don't* make unhealthy choices" tells your brain that it's your own personal will that drives the decision. It's an affirmation of you making the choice. It gives a feeling of empowerment, boosts your endorphins, and gives you a subconscious feeling of control that gives you the extra push to walk away from the dessert.

Saying "I can't" shows your brain that it's external forces—not you—dictating what you want. Using words that show ownership over the decision doubles the success rate. Understanding and accepting that you are in charge of how and what you think and behave is powerful.

Right now, I want you to think about ways you've shrunk yourself down or disguised yourself to fit everyone else's ideas. We try so hard to play by the rules, a strict—but somehow arbitrary—set of principles, which we feel we have to abide by to be worthy. We are constantly striving to, quite frankly, "be enough." Smart enough, strong enough, good enough.

Just the other day, one of the entrepreneurs in my Intentional CEO program asked me how she could know when she's "done enough." I told her, "Enough is like a bucket with a hole in it—it's never filled." If you are constantly chasing some imaginary finish line that you can never reach, it's no wonder you end your days exhausted and feeling like you should have done more.

In our mind, there's some magical set of checkboxes we have to tick in order to be *good enough*.

ARE YOU QUALIFIED?

Here's an upsetting fact: Most women won't apply for a job unless they meet 100 percent of the qualifications. They feel they need to check every single box before they submit their résumé. Men, on the other hand require, on average, meeting only 60 percent of the qualifications. Even when women are more than qualified, a vast number seem to struggle to deem themselves experts in their field.*

In my research into this phenomenon, I came across many great examples of how women tend to shy away from expert status, but one in particular stood out to me, and I want to share it with you.

It's an anecdote a former senior executive shared with the *New York Times* as to why more women aren't reaching CEO status in larger corporations. In the article she talks about how women often fail to see themselves as experts. She relayed the story of a presenter at a conference who asked any breastfeeding experts in the crowd to identify themselves. In that large room, packed full of people, one "man raised his hand [saying] he had watched his wife for three months. The women in the crowd, mothers among them, didn't come forward as experts."

You and I both know there were women in that audience who had fought with their breast pumps in the tiny stalls of their company bathrooms during their lunch breaks; that there were mothers in that room who had read stacks and stacks of books on breastfeeding late into the night until their eyes blurred the words on the pages; that there were certainly women in that audience who had years of experience holding their own children to their breasts. And yet none of them considered themselves an expert. Just one man in the audience felt qualified.

The article noted that "many women, accomplished as they are, don't feel the same sense of innate confidence as their male peers." For a long time this was referred to as the "confidence gap," and it was touted as evidence that women suffer from low self-esteem. But new findings show it's not confidence—it's rule-following that holds us back. As former CEO of DuPont, Ellen Kullman confided, "We [women] are never taught to fight for ourselves. I think we tend to be brought up thinking

---

* Please know that this research in no way is meant to pose men and women against one another. We don't rise by stepping on others; we rise by lifting together. I'm merely using these examples to show how women think differently than men in many instances.

that life's fair, that you thrive and deliver, and the rest will take care of itself."

PLAYING BY THE RULES

According to Hannah Riley Bowles of Harvard's Kennedy School, a leading expert on how gender influences pay, "Women do seem to toot their horn less than their male colleagues. The problem is when you stop there and say, 'Okay well, women just need to be more like men.' The story of why women are more modest than men is much more complicated than that." In fact, women tend to be penalized by others for boasting, so many shy away from it.

This is true even when it's not really boasting, but just identifying yourself in a certain way. I've noticed this myself in conversations I've had with women regarding terms like *girl boss*, *lady boss*, or *boss babe*. What's wrong with just being the boss? We don't call men *boy boss* or *boss hunk*.* Why is there this need among many women to soften the title?

I've found that women either love that word, *boss*, and embrace it (as I do), or they bristle at it. When I dove deeper into this with the members of my community, I got to the heart of the problem. The word *boss* conjures up the word *bossy*—a word none of us liked to be called as children.

Here's the thing: no one calls little boys "bossy"—they call them "overconfident." Only girls are bossy . . . girls who are then redirected and told to be nice and play by the rules. This is why girls tend to succeed more in school than boys do—schools are built for people who play by the rules. Life, however, is not built the same.

I'm not saying you need to stop playing by the rules. I'm just saying that rules are meant to be challenged. Do you play by this rule: you can only achieve a certain level if you attend thousands of hours of training?

---

* Please tell me that you snickered a bit when you read "boss hunk." Seriously, for just one minute, imagine reading a CEO's bio where he describes himself as a boss hunk, and now think about how you are perceived if you are calling yourself a boss babe.

Or that you can be taken seriously only if you have a certain set of letters after your name? That rule isn't always true and needs to be challenged.

Obviously you cannot set up shop as a doctor or lawyer without some of those fancy letters and diplomas, but what's holding you back from identifying yourself as you truly want to be described?

Artist · Author · Dancer · Entrepreneur
Musician · Athlete · Painter · Baker
Photographer · Breastfeeding Expert*

What is keeping you from identifying yourself as you aspire to be? I'm guessing you've seen this in your friends. Maybe your good friend is a gifted storyteller with dreams of one day publishing her work, but she hesitates to move forward on that dream because she doesn't think she can call herself a writer. She hides behind the excuse, "I don't get paid to do this full-time, so I can't call myself an author."

But a writer is simply *someone who writes.* They don't have to be listed on the *New York Times* Best Sellers List or even have their work published to earn that title. In fact, many authors are self-published, and there's not a ton of room on those bestseller lists.

The only difference between the woman who dreams of being a writer and the author of your favorite book is that at some point along the way, that author chose to stop allowing self-doubt to creep into her narrative and started calling herself a writer.

I remember when I added the title of *author* to my own list. It felt a little like imposter syndrome—even though I had published a book! I questioned it for a few minutes, my finger hovered above the Submit key because it felt like maybe it wasn't real. But I punched the button and decided to own it. When we step into the path we really desire—even though it's something we really want—it can feel uncomfortable. Discomfort shows us that we are growing; it's a sign that we are breaking old patterns and pushing ourselves into something new.

---

* You know I couldn't resist adding that one in here!

SET YOUR INTENTIONS

Start associating yourself with the type of person you want to be—if you want to be an entrepreneur, start calling yourself an entrepreneur.* You have to believe in *you* before anyone else will. Using a title or an identity that reinforces that belief shows others your intentions.

It's no wonder people unknowingly insult you by calling you a hobbyist when you dream of making your passion into a full-time career. It's no surprise that they don't take your big dreams seriously. After all, you don't—not if you are choosing to use words that don't communicate your intentions. Own it, put a sign on your door, change your social media profile, do whatever it is you need to do to show everyone else that you and your dreams are significant.

We give in, though, to imposter syndrome. The thing that was keeping my finger hovering over that Submit button is the same thing that holds women back time and time again. Worried that we aren't playing by the rules—that at some point, we'll be exposed and everyone around us will figure out we don't actually belong—we underestimate our experience and our expertise simply because we don't check *all* the boxes of what we think qualifies us.

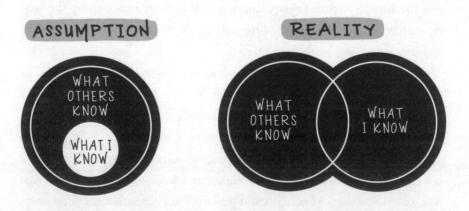

ASSUMPTION

WHAT OTHERS KNOW

WHAT I KNOW

REALITY

WHAT OTHERS KNOW

WHAT I KNOW

---

* And start hanging out with *successful* entrepreneurs. Note that I said "successful," meaning that they aren't just talking about it, but are actively working on their businesses.

WHO AM I REALLY?

Imposter syndrome is a rational response to irrationally assessing our own abilities. You see, our ruler for measuring ourselves is not very accurate. We set ourselves up with expectations we would never place on anyone else because we aren't able to truly step outside of ourselves and assess our strengths. In other words, we tend to undervalue what we know, what we've learned, and what we are capable of accomplishing. We are basically choosing to toss out the evidence—the breadcrumbs of our past—that show us we are qualified.

Without evidence, there are three options:

1. You can choose to believe that you are amazing at what you do.
2. You can choose to believe that you are terrible at what you do and quit.
3. You can choose to believe that you are terrible at what you do but are somehow successful in fooling everyone into believing you are amazing.

Very few people choose option one. Most of us stick with number three. And when I say most of us, we can include Maya Angelou, who once said to herself (after writing her eleventh book), "Uh-oh, they're going to find out now. I've run a game on everybody."

We can also include Jodie Foster, who said she thought it was a fluke that she'd gotten into Yale and that she won the Academy Award and that they'd come and take the Oscar back. They'd come to her house, knock on the door, and say, "Excuse me, we meant to give that to someone else. That was going to Meryl Streep."

Meryl Streep who, by the way, has said, "Why would anyone want to see me again in a movie? I don't know how to act anyway." Never mind that she's been nominated for more Oscars than anyone in history. It's theorized that up to 70 percent of people experience imposter syndrome. Based on what we just read, though, I think it's something more like this:

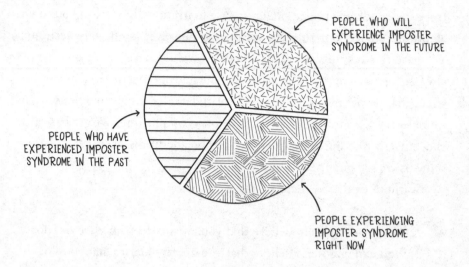

PEOPLE WHO WILL EXPERIENCE IMPOSTER SYNDROME IN THE FUTURE

PEOPLE WHO HAVE EXPERIENCED IMPOSTER SYNDROME IN THE PAST

PEOPLE EXPERIENCING IMPOSTER SYNDROME RIGHT NOW

We all feel, at times, like the clothes we wear are really just costumes designed to convince people we are responsible adults, when deep inside we feel like kids playing dress-up in our parents' closet. That's the big secret to adulthood—we all see ourselves in the mirror as twelve-year-olds wearing responsibilities that feel three sizes too big. We think everyone around us has it all together, when we are all fighting the imposter syndrome that's nipping at our heels.

THE CONSTANT RACE FOR ACHIEVEMENT

Mary Marantz is a Yale Law School graduate and the first in her immediate family to go to college. Growing up in rural West Virginia in a single-wide trailer with mushrooms carpeting the floor, she constantly felt the intense pressure to rise above her beginnings. It was quietly playing next to her at the age of five as she toiled through workbooks for kids twice her age; it zigzagged alongside her as she climbed up the rock pile in her backyard. Being anything less than flawless was never an option.

When it came to her dad, there was never any question as to what was expected of Mary. "I really do think he believed for anybody in the outside world to give me a shot . . . I was gonna have to be twice as good," she shared with me. "I was . . . not going to give them a reason to exclude me." Acceptance was hinged on the high price of constant achievement.

So often we talk about grit and perseverance as badges of honor, but as Mary says, "There's also a shadow side . . . that says: I will always be in it alone. I will never have the help that I need. I will always have to do it myself . . . And if I do go out and fall short . . . then I won't be worthy of love."

What's funny is that in the race for constant achievement, we have this idea that we cannot stop, we cannot let them see us sweat. So we keep striving, we keep hustling. We are so busy looking at our feet, doing our best to not fall down, that we don't look up and see all those women next to us who are panting, trying to catch their breath, running alongside us thinking the same damn thing.

We set an unachievable bar for ourselves that we wouldn't hold for anyone else. And we abuse ourselves mercilessly when we don't sail over it with ease.

We call ourselves lazy for not getting up at 4 a.m. because an article we read once told us that successful people do seventy-five things before their kids get up. We berate ourselves and say "I'm never enough" when just moments before we criticized ourselves for being "too much" for the people around us. We define ourselves with words we would never use to describe anyone else.

Mary has learned that "words have the power to either speak life or speak death. When they call you smart, you act smart. You rise and fall to what is expected of you."

She is absolutely right. We rise and fall like the tide based on what everyone else thinks. It's time to describe ourselves instead of waiting like a damsel in distress to be saved by the words of others. We can choose the words that define us; we can allow the words we want to speak life into us, rather than waiting to hear them from someone else.

Truthfully, it doesn't matter who you've been in the past. What matters is who you become. And that happens by making a choice: choosing who you want to be and stepping into it fully and authentically.

EVERY LITTLE WORD

Even the adjectives you use to describe what you do—those define you. Are you a speaker or a highly sought-after speaker? Are you a business owner or a successful entrepreneur? Are you a writer or an acclaimed author?

Dynamic • Energetic • Industrious
Skillful • Ingenious • Perceptive

Your words matter.

As a matter of fact, go right now and look over your professional bio or résumé. Read it as if you were a stranger and then ask yourself if you would hire you. If not, it's time for a rewrite. I've got a whole list of words like the ones above and some advice on describing yourself in the free reader's guide that comes with this book. You can find it in the Resources section of my website at TanyaDalton.com.

Here's the truth: sometimes in order to realize our true impact, we have to stop feeling small. Too often we underestimate our ideas or the words we say, and we don't think we can make that much of a difference. But it's the little things that can set off a chain reaction much bigger than ourselves.

You've possibly heard me talk in the past about the domino effect, and how a single domino can knock over another one that's 50 percent bigger than itself with just a little momentum.* By lining your dominos up, you can knock over a domino thousands of feet tall. The same is true for our actions and the words we say—they can have more significance than we think.

---

* If you have my book *The Joy of Missing Out*, you can dive further into the domino effect in chapter 8.

We have to change the way we look at the impact we can have on others. I'm going to give you the same advice someone once gave me, the advice that—in my mind—changed everything. Are you ready?

You are being selfish.

Ouch. That hurts. As someone who prides herself on always giving to others, that slap in the face stung a bit.* Maybe it stings for you too . . . but it's true.

When you hold yourself back from sharing your gifts with others, when you and your beautifully unique gifts are not shared because you are too busy shrinking back, you are keeping others from receiving your message. When you choose to play small and define yourself with words that don't allow you to accept the greatness you are capable of, you are being selfish.

YOUR BLAST RADIUS

I know what you are thinking: *Yeah, that's true if you have a bunch of followers or if you are famous.* But it's true for people like you and me too. Even famous people started like us—just normal people. "Normal" being a relative term here.

You have the potential to touch the lives of about 80,000 people. *You.* Go back and read that number again: 80,000.

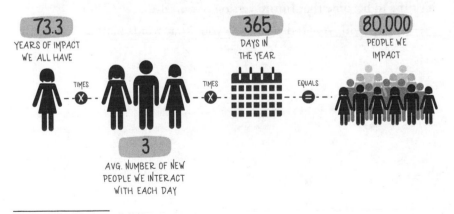

---

* Seems ironic, don't you think?

I'm not much on math, but let me break it down a bit for you. The average person lives for 78.3 years, but most of us don't remember much before the age of 5, so we'll make our "years of impact" 73.3. We can assume that we interact with an average of three new people a day—from the grocery clerk ringing up our milk to the neighbor down the street with the dog that never stops barking to the other parents cheering their kids on at the soccer field—some days we meet more, some days less, but three is about average. With 365 days in a year (multiplied by our 73.3 years), that means we are able to connect with over 80,000 people in our lifetime.

More than you thought, right? More than I thought too. So the question is: If you possibly touch 80,000 lives in your lifetime, do you want to have a positive impact or do you want to keep thinking of yourself as small? This is a choice—one you can actively choose simply by redefining how you look at yourself.

You have a great deal of influence over your world and the worlds of others. It doesn't matter if you are famous or have a big platform—each of us has the ability to affect and change lives. We may start small, but that doesn't mean we have to think small.

Anyone can step into their purpose and make an impact. Even if you don't think you can, trust me—it's possible. What if we flipped the phrase "fake it until you make it" to "believe it until you become it"?

And now that we know that what we tell ourselves is what we believe, it's time to become that future version of ourselves.

It starts with you and ends with you. Your words matter.

LIES THAT HOLD YOU BACK:

- I can't catch a break.
- Who am I to think I can do something big?
- What difference can I make?
- No one believes in me.

TRUTHS THAT MOVE YOU FORWARD:

- When I clearly ask for what I want, I can get what I want.
- I will impact the lives of 80,000 people in a positive way.
- I will put myself out there even if I don't think I fulfill all the qualifications.
- When I talk about myself with confidence, others see me differently.

SPRINGBOARD: Start identifying yourself as you want others to see you. Use the word bank in the Interactive Reader's Guide to update your résumé and/or bio.

part two

PROJECTION

Answers the Question: What?

three

CHOOSE TO SEE YOUR FUTURE

My world changed in 2008 on a hot summer evening in Dallas—one of those Texas days where the temperature doesn't dip below ninety degrees until you are dead asleep in your bed late at night. My kids, though, were used to the sticky heat and were swinging on the jungle gym in the backyard. I could hear their shouts and giggles as the phone on the wall in my kitchen rang out.*

I quickly grabbed the phone because I knew, without hesitation, it would be John calling me. At that time in our lives, he was working in international marketing for large Fortune 500 companies. He would sometimes go on marathon trips around the world, touching almost every continent in one fell swoop, so we had a system back then. We would talk for a few minutes each morning and again each evening—just as one of us was getting up and the other was winding down their day. This made us feel close even half a world away from each other.

I don't remember where exactly he was calling from on that day, to be

---

* Remember when we had phones attached to the walls instead of shoved in our back pockets? I had to remind my kids of that when I read them this story. And yes, it made me feel old.

totally honest—it was always hard to keep track of where he was because he jumped from country to country so often—but I can vividly recall the conversation we had that evening.

I can remember sitting on the steps in the kitchen that still smelled of grilled cheese sandwiches, feeling the hard wall on my back as I leaned against it, looking out the window to watch Jack and Kate chasing each other up and down the slide. I can remember every detail of that minute in my life because that was the moment that changed me.

Our conversation started out as most of them did, with me doing most of the chatting. (I always say John married me so he didn't have to talk too much.) I was laughing about the new phrase Kate had uttered just that morning and how Jack had thought it was so funny he'd grabbed his tummy when he giggled uncontrollably.

That's when I realized that John had gone silent.

So silent that I would have thought our connection had broken if it weren't for the fact that I could hear him breathing in low, deep breaths. Worried, I asked him what was the matter, only to be met with complete silence. At this point I was alarmed, and I asked him urgently what was going on. After a full minute of silence, I heard him sigh and dolefully say, "I'm missing everything." It took him so long to say those three words, each one seemed to be its own sentence.

I lightheartedly tried to put his fears at ease, saying that the kids would be excited to see him when he got back, but it didn't seem to comfort him. You see, my husband is an amazing father. He loves nothing more than to have the four of us together, and to know that his marathon business trips were tugging at his heart so strongly just about broke me. I did my best to comfort him, but I could tell he wasn't really convinced.

Ten minutes later, I stood to hang up the phone, and a choice was made. I decided that the little side-hobby business I had started with fifty dollars was going to drastically change the lives of my family. I set a big dream in motion standing there in the middle of my bright-yellow kitchen. I was going to grow my business so that my husband could leave corporate America behind and come and work alongside me. I would absorb his MBA income and create the life we really wanted for our family. Me. A bold choice for a girl with two small kids and zero business experience.

Suddenly, though, I could see a much different future than I ever had before.

BUILDING YOUR CATHEDRAL

When you think about it, when you imagine your future self, you are basically starting with the end in mind. Thinking far off into the future allows you to let go of current realities, roadblocks, and obligations and allows you to think bigger than today. It gives you permission to say yes to the big, audacious dreams and untethers you from whatever it is that's grabbing ahold of your ankles and keeping you from achieving great heights. This is Cathedral Thinking—dreaming, planning, and creating blueprints that reach far into the future.

Cathedral Thinking is a centuries-old concept adopted by architects, artisans, and planners who contributed to great works designed to live well past their own lifetimes. The grand Duomo di Firenze is a beautiful example of Cathedral Thinking; no matter where you walk along the stony streets of Florence, Italy, its iconic spire can be seen towering over the rooftops.

It's hard to pinpoint when exactly the majestic duomo was built; we could say it was 1296, when construction first began, but the dome we all recognize wasn't added until the 1400s, and the exterior wasn't considered complete until 1886. Almost 600 years in the making, the city planners knew the morning they broke ground that they would never see the completed cathedral in all her glory. But that didn't matter—it was bigger than them or their lifetimes.

They began with the end in mind.

Your Cathedral doesn't have to be your own vision to have value. It can be joining a cause or an organization that's working toward a greater good. Think about the space program in the 1950s and '60s—all those people, who knew they would never reach the moon themselves, committed toward that shared dream. Some risked their lives testing the sound barrier, others made dangerous trips to the different layers of the atmosphere, while many did their part by calculating and crunching numbers on their slide rules, all using their unique gifts working toward the common cause. Every one of them knew that they themselves wouldn't put their feet on the lunar surface, but they did it because they had the end in mind—getting a person on the moon. And even that is not the full Cathedral built and finished. We are working now to get a person on Mars thanks to that moon landing.

Cathedral Thinking can look different to each of us and what we want our legacy to be, but they all "require the same foundation: a far-reaching vision, a well thought-out blueprint, and a . . . commitment to long-term implementation." Your Cathedral doesn't have to be fifty or a hundred years in the making. It's simply the idea that, when we think with the future in mind, we stretch beyond ourselves today and create a legacy steeped in purpose.[*]

Cathedrals can be anything that's a far-reaching vision:

- Start a foundation
- Retire at 50
- Achieve complete financial independence
- Reach C-level in my company
- Live on my own private island
- Live an active lifestyle well into my nineties
- Write a bestselling book series

What's important is to not get caught up in what your Cathedral is *supposed* to be. This is not a beauty pageant where you will score extra points with the judges for talking about world peace. It's okay if your

---

[*] I want to take a minute to remind you of the definition of *purpose* we agreed upon in the introduction—purpose is working toward a larger good. Don't get stuck worrying about the weight of purpose and instead focus on what you want in your long-term.

Cathedral is about growing a conscious company, achieving a personal dream, or creating a family legacy.

Your Cathedral can be anything that is important to *you*, that fits well with your values and purpose. What we are looking for here is a bigger, more significant target to focus our lives toward.

Leapfrogging from one goal to the next seems like a fun way to gamify life, but if there's no higher purpose to connect them, the achievements will no longer fulfill us after a time. The feeling we get when we accomplish a goal is fleeting. We get a high and then it passes—it's temporary. The only way to feel it again is to "win" again, so we are constantly wearing ourselves out chasing after new wins.

If our vision is bigger and focused on the long-term, though, our daily lives can feel more meaningful—the feeling of winning stretches like taffy and clings to us every day. I don't know about you, but I want some of that. I want to end my days knowing I'm working and moving toward something bigger. I want to slip into my bed at night feeling satisfied and pleasantly fulfilled.

YOU, MATT DAMON, AND NATALIE PORTMAN WALK INTO A BAR . . .

Too often we are so busy living in our day-to-day lives that we forget we can look out past today's horizon and see a bigger future. Focused on checking off the tasks from our never-ending to-do list, we don't stop to ask ourselves, *Where am I going?*

It's understandable that the future is hard for us to see. After all, there is a clear disconnect between who we are today and who we will become. To me, this is the biggest secret to understanding how to unlock your potential: realizing that your brain sees your future self and other people exactly the same way—as strangers.

UCLA psychologist Hal Hershfield has led a number of studies to illustrate how our brain disconnects with our future selves. In my favorite study of his, he used an fMRI machine to map brain activity shifts when people imagined themselves in the present (present you) versus thinking of themselves in the future (future you).

The researchers looked at the two parts of the brain that are most active when we think about ourselves. They discovered that these parts of the brain would light up brighter when the volunteers thought of themselves today rather than when they thought of themselves in the future.

Here's what's most interesting, though: when subjects described themselves ten years from now, their brain activity was the same as it was when they were describing Matt Damon or Natalie Portman. In other words, our future self feels like someone else . . . like a stranger we kinda know.

I find this fascinating because it clearly explains why we choose the cookie over the carrot, why we splurge on the shoes we cannot afford over saving in our 401(k), why we choose the immediate gratification over the long-term success. You, in the future, is not you! (At least to your brain it's not.)

So why not give in to immediate gratification? Why worry about saving for the retirement account? After all, to your brain, you don't have to deal with the repercussions. Some stranger who looks and acts and happens to have the same name as you—she's the one who will have to deal with the mess. Not you.

HOW MUCH KETCHUP WILL YOU DRINK?

It seems crazy, doesn't it? I know that right now you are thinking there's no way that you treat the future version of yourself exactly as you would a stranger on the street,* so let me continue to nerd-out on the studies and share another one with you, because this understanding is key to unlocking why we struggle to see ourselves in the future. This one is by Princeton psychologist Emily Pronin, who led an experiment in which participants

---

* Even if that stranger does happen to be showcased buying bulk toilet paper in the "Stars! They're Just Like Us" section of your magazine.

were fooled into believing that they were studying reactions to a gross mixture of ketchup and soy sauce. In reality, the researchers were actually studying the relationship between the volunteers and their future selves.

Divided into three groups, the participants were told that they would be able to control how much of the disgusting drink would be consumed. Group 1 was told they would be choosing for themselves how much to drink that day, Group 2 would be choosing for someone else, and Group 3 would also be choosing for themselves . . . *but they wouldn't have to choke down the concoction for two whole weeks.*

As you can imagine, Group 1, who was told they were choosing for themselves, opted for the tiniest amount to down that day—about a teaspoon. The second group who was choosing for a stranger made a bolder choice; they chose the largest amount for that other person to stomach—a quarter cup. Why not? *They* didn't have to drink it! But the third group—the ones who were choosing for themselves in 14 days? They *also* chose the largest amount—a full quarter cup of the revolting concoction for their future selves to guzzle down!

As the lead researcher noted, "In the present, you're very aware of your feelings, but in the future, it's more abstract." *You* are not *you* in the future. Scary, strange, but true—and empowering. Now that we know that we have this misconception of believing our future self is a different person, we can change that relationship. And that starts by seeing a future with you in it.

SEEING YOUR FUTURE

Do you remember your first job interview? Odds are stacked pretty high that the person sitting across the desk from you in the ill-fitting suit asked the loaded question, "Where do you see yourself in ten years?" The problem was, you didn't even know what you were having for lunch in two hours, let alone what life would look like 3,650 days down the road!

In fact, you may be thinking to yourself right now: *I have* no *idea what*

I truly want for the future. This is one of the most common stumbling blocks I hear from the women in my programs and in my community. They want to dream of the future, but they have no idea how.

So often we end up living the way we think we are *supposed* to live, chasing other people's dreams or whatever it is we think we should be doing. In the pursuit of adulting, we can lose sight of the bright future we once dreamed of having. We are so busy worrying about paying the rent that we let go of the old ideals and dreams, thinking it's silly to hope we will ever be able to pursue them.

Adulting is just an excuse people use to let go of their big dreams—you can be responsible *and* you can pursue a brighter future for yourself. It's not replacing one with the other—it's both living in harmony in your life.

Remember back in the first chapter when we agreed that if you want to move forward, you need to begin by looking back? Projection is when we see the fruits of that deep reflection work.

Let's be real; looking at a blank page and trying to fill it with ideas for the future feels like an incredibly daunting task. It would be easy to throw up our hands and say, "This is just too hard." But when we use our past, we aren't really starting with a blank page. We have an entire library filled with our history, a lifetime to delve into. We can use water from that well in our past to draw from.

Reflection creates a foundation for projection and helps you discover some motivators in your life that answer the question of what (and why) you do what you do. Let's peel back some of the layers of the past, just a bit, and help you see your future. It starts by asking a couple of questions.

Question 1: What Are Your Lost Dreams?

When we were young we all had big, lofty ideas of what was possible. Maybe you proudly told everyone you met that you were going to be an astronaut or the president. Or perhaps you dreamed of being a superhero.

Okay, we can agree that becoming Wonder Woman is probably out of the question, but, I mean, who doesn't want an invisible plane and a magic lasso? Hold on a minute, though. Before you laugh at that old dream, let's

ADULTING:

an *excuse* people use to
let go of their big dreams.

take a deeper look at it. Why did you want to become Wonder Woman? Was it because she stood for justice? Or because she helped find truth when others couldn't? Did you love that she inspired a generation of girls to be strong and independent? Start asking that meaningful question *why*.

Look at the career you dreamed of and ask yourself: What about that job sounded amazing? Who were the people I looked up to? What qualities did they embody that made me admire them? Think about the activities you looked forward to with anticipation. I'm not talking about the piano lessons your mom dragged you to, fighting and screaming; I'm talking about the ones you anticipated with excitement. What was appealing to you? If it was playing softball, was it the sport itself or was it the competition? Or the teamwork? Or the exercise and skill it required? Don't just ask yourself why—dig deeper and ask it again four more times.

I did this exercise of using reflection to create projection with one of my clients. Amy Bridges has her master's degree in education and has spent most of her professional life teaching and developing educational software, but she also fills her time with volunteer work, church activities, and music. When we met to talk, she said she was ready to "ignite the passion that helps me feel like I have a purpose."

That's what I like to hear.

We dove headfirst into her childhood and when she reflected back, she shared that her time was spent building and creating, playing, and devouring books to learn. Going to church was never something she felt forced to do because she loved being around other people. She loved playing games with the kids in her neighborhood, *school* being one of her favorites as she always played the teacher.

Knowing that she is in the education industry, I asked if she always wanted to be a teacher or something different. She laughed and said she wanted to be a county extension agent,* which, she explained, is "essentially

---

* Yes, your reaction was the same as mine. County *what*?! I learned that county extension agents work with groups to facilitate discussions and develop educational programs to meet local needs, and they typically focus on agriculture and natural resources.

a 4-H leader." And when I prodded about why, she mused, "I think I always wanted to be in a position to help people in lots of ways, not necessarily in a classroom." We talked about the peaks and valleys of her life map, and Amy noticed that the high points in her life were consistently revolving around being with other people—sometimes with family, other times volunteering or in acts of service.

As Amy started revisiting her childhood out loud, we both could see some strong threads connecting her past to her present, along with some common themes emerging, which suddenly became obvious. We noticed themes of supporting and educating others, using creativity, and finding solutions.

I asked her if that was more true to who she really was, rather than the data-driven way she had always thought of herself. That seemed like a lightbulb moment for Amy. "You know," she admitted, "I love that idea of creativity . . . I think that when you have a degree in math, you think of yourself as logical and analytical. But the idea that I can take those things that I love to do and move them into new creative places to still be able to help others is going to make for a pretty good mission statement." Now she is giving her purpose a solid definition.

While we don't want to dwell on the past or get caught up in what might have been, we do want to see what resonated deep inside of us before we had the filter of adulthood. We can discover some compelling clues as to who it is we want to become, and we can uncover some of what we don't want, which is even more powerful.

Question 2: Can You Spin a Negative into a Positive?

I'm not going to lie, looking into your past isn't always full of sunshine and lollipops. There are some dark, cobwebby corners and damp areas that reek with the sharp smell of rot. But we're going to need to shine some light into those areas to get to what we really want. Or, to use a term we talked about earlier, we'll need to dig deep with both hands into that pile of manure so we can find the pony. We need to get some real answers, even when they're difficult to find or even accept.

This is often why we will do just about anything to avoid the "deep work"—peeling back the layers and taking a peek. We are afraid of what we might see—or what we might expose. If you were sitting next to me right now, I would look you in the eye and admit this is not easy. I know sometimes the truth can sting a little bit (or a lot), but it's when we pull back those bandages on those old wounds that we really start to heal.

That is when we start to see growth: when we look at the hard things, the ugly parts, the things we don't want to think about, the things we don't really like. The only way to change and grow is to acknowledge the hard things. That's how we can become resilient.

The American Psychological Association defines "resilience" not as coping with the negative but as "adapting well in the face of adversity, trauma, tragedy, threats or significant sources of stress." *Adapting.* Not conquering or overcoming or even combatting—adapting. We can adapt *and* we can take that definition a step further: resilience is the ability to acknowledge and accept our own shortcomings and use that knowledge to our advantage.

Let me show you how. Did you know that of all the emotions, people try hardest to avoid regret? We can handle anger, frustration, and resentment, but we will do just about anything to avoid regret. That's a powerful tool to understand, because we can use it to get in touch with our future selves.

If regret clarifies what we want to avoid, let's flip it on its head to discover what we want to attract. Think about this: How would it feel twelve months from now if everything we regretted was turned upside down? We would feel the opposite of regret. We would feel resilient satisfaction, fulfillment. Isn't that what Cathedral Thinking is all about? Looking at our future and finding those things that bring satisfaction, that bring us that happiness?

Take a piece of paper and divide it into two columns. In the first, write down your regrets that you uncovered when you reflected back. List them all out, and then I want you to write down the exact opposite of each of them in the second column.

REGRET TO RESILIENCE

WORKED LATE EVERY NIGHT LAST WEEK ⟶ LEAVE WORK BY 4PM AT LEAST TWICE A WEEK

STAYED ANGRY AT MY FRIEND AFTER A FIGHT ⟶ FOCUS ON FORGIVENESS AND LETTING GO

DIDN'T SPEND ENOUGH TIME WITH MY KIDS ⟶ CALL FAMILY MEETING TO BRAINSTORM ACTIVITIES

When you know what you *don't* want, it's easier to see what you do.

ROCK BOTTOM IS JUST A PLACE TO START

"I hit a rock-bottom low . . . and I knew it couldn't possibly get worse."

Most happy-ending stories begin on a brighter note with something like *Once upon a time*, but not every story begins the same way.

For Amy Lacey, founding Cali'flour Foods didn't start off like a fairy tale. Her multimillion-dollar company grew its roots from a much darker place filled with pain, depression, and a lot of negativity in her life.

So often we think of rock bottom as a deep, dark trench where life barely survives, like the lonely chasms at the bottom of the ocean. But when the world hands you a negative, you can choose to push back and find the positive seed you can plant and grow.

When talking about that time in her life, Amy said, "When it feels like the whole world is falling in, you have to remember that this too shall pass. And I'm grateful for the hardship because it gave me the confidence to know what's possible." The word *hardship* doesn't fully embody the journey that brought Amy full circle to founding her business.

Long before her company was even a glimmer of an idea, Amy wasn't really sure what was possible in her life. For a while, she desperately questioned if anything was actually possible. She spent years fighting a mysterious illness that left her needing multiple surgeries and completely bedridden for nine continuous months. It's no surprise she found herself in a deep, dark place thinking she didn't have much to offer her husband and three kids.

When she was finally diagnosed with both lupus and Sjögren's syndrome, it helped to put a name to the illness, but it didn't change how she felt physically. "My body was attacking me with inflammation, and I needed to make it stop," she told me. Amy decided to focus on one thing she could control—the food she put in to fuel her body. Amy cleared her diet, stopped eating processed foods and cut out all grains and gluten, and saw an immediate improvement.

And while she physically felt better, mentally she worried that her new eating lifestyle would cause a lot of disruption for her family. At first glance, it seemed that family activities like their Friday Night Pizza Night were doomed.

Determined to not regret missing out on any of the fun, she decided she needed to find a way to join in on the tradition. "I wanted to bring some normalcy back to my family. We used to have so much fun, and I wanted to get that back."

There were no options at the grocery store or anywhere else, so Amy and her daughter decided it was up to them to create something unique—a pizza crust made from cauliflower with absolutely no fillers. There were lots of test recipes and failed attempts, but she finally achieved a crust that not only she liked but her kids did too.

Friday nights were restored, and Amy finally felt better than she had in years. She told me, "I was proactive and feeling better and that helped my family be better. And then it went into serving others to be better too— others who were really feeling hopeless just as I had felt. I knew that if I could overcome it, they could too."

She started making her pizzas and selling them at the farmers market where she quickly sold out week after week. Next she expanded to selling online and at a couple of local grocery stores. She poured every bit of her savings into the business, getting it off the ground—purchasing huge, expensive equipment and renting a commercial kitchen. By the end of 2016, she was deeply in debt, but she kept hearing story after story from ecstatic pizza lovers telling her how their health had been transformed by her crust.

Amy started sharing the testimonials and transformations, and almost instantly her pizza went viral. "We went from negative $269,000 in sales to $5.3 million in 12 months. And a mere two years later, [we were making] almost $21 million. Online, we were selling a pizza crust every three seconds."

Amy is widely recognized as being one of the first to start the cauliflower health movement. Hundreds of thousands of people have had their health impacted positively simply because she chose to spin her negative into something good for the world.

Regret and frustration are easier to pinpoint and push against when we turn our pain into a positive projection; that's when it shifts into creative pain. That's when it bursts into something brand new and becomes a powerful way to start to view a new future for yourself.

BECOME YOUR OWN HERO

It's important to realize we are the hero in our own story. We have the ability, with the perspective of time, to see our past as fertile ground to plant seeds for our future. We can choose to allow it to define us, or we can choose to be our own authors and use our experiences.

Nora Ephron is a name you may not be familiar with, but you probably know her films, like *Sleepless in Seattle* or *When Harry Met Sally*. As a woman in the male-dominated movie business, she was a rare triple threat as a writer, director, and producer. She also had an amazing knack for telling something like it is and putting a funny spin on it at the same time.

Much of Nora's writing could be classified as nonfiction fiction because it was so tied to her real life. As she put it, "Why would anyone write fiction when what actually happens is so amazing?"

"Take notes," her mom, a successful screenwriter, often advised her as a child. "Everything is copy." In other words, anything and everything that happens to you can be considered fodder for a story or a punchline. When Nora was bullied at school, had her bike stolen, or dealt with a horrible teacher, her parents would simply say: "It's all copy."

Nora explained, "When you slip on a banana peel, people laugh at you. But when you *tell* people you slipped on a banana peel, it's your laugh. So you become the hero, rather than the victim of the joke."

Ultimately, no matter the outcome, you win because it's *your* story to craft. And that story is something you can learn from and can feel okay sharing because, well, we all slip on a banana peel from time to time. Don't we?

It's a very different way of looking at things, if you ask me. We don't have to be the victims of our stories, of the bad situations and the challenges we are faced with—we can choose to look at them from a different perspective.

Everything in Nora Ephron's life was copy. She shared a lot of her personal struggles in her stories and in her movies—from her messy divorce to navigating the aging process. All of it is copy for us to use in projecting what we want our future to look like.

You can own your story too. You can be the heroine even in the midst of struggle and tragedy. All you have to do is remember that everything is copy and a future of possibilities becomes so much easier to see.

We need to choose to see our future with us in it; that will help connect our decisions of today to the future we want.

For me, standing in my sunny kitchen, hanging up the phone after that pivotal phone call with John, I could see the future so clearly, it made my decision easy. I could have questioned it and second-guessed my abilities, but I didn't. I saw the future I wanted, so I pulled out a notebook and laid out my plans right there at my kitchen table while the evening light streamed in and my kids played at my feet.

I wrote out ideas, designed streamlined systems, and organized, stopping only for a short time to bathe the kids and tuck them into bed. I kissed them both quickly that night with no extra bedtime stories because I was already itching to get back downstairs. I had a future formulating in my head, and I couldn't rest until I mapped it out on paper.

Within about a year, that future became my reality. John was able to permanently leave the corporate world behind forever and come and work with me at the business I had created. Today we don't work side by side. Instead we sit across the desk from each other, laughing, planning, and working together just as I once dreamed we would.

Your future is yours to write, so let's create a plan to make that future happen.

LIES THAT HOLD US BACK:

- I just live for today and don't worry about tomorrow.
- I am damaged.
- I have no idea what the future looks like for me.
- I'm too old to do anything new.

TRUTHS THAT MOVE US FORWARD:

- When I think about my future, I can clearly see it's connected to my choices today.
- I've had bad things happen in the past, but I can use those experiences as fuel for my future.
- I can reconnect with my past and see that my childhood dreams are possible.
- I am the hero of my own story, and I have the ability to use my experience to my advantage.

SPRINGBOARD: Fill out the Regret to Resilience chart in the Interactive Reader's Guide.

four

CHOOSE TO FIND YOUR FOCUS

Have you ever stood in the middle of a grocery store frantically running through the list in your head, doing your best to remember what you came in to grab in the first place? Or maybe you've had a time or two (or ten) where you have forgotten which day of the week it is? We all forget things from time to time; it happens to all of us.

On the outside Amy Jo Martin had the kind of life that looked perfect in the little three-inch squares of social media. She was riding the wave of success with her first company—which hit seven figures within two years—some of the biggest brands and movie stars in the world were working directly with her, and she had a *New York Times* bestselling book on the shelves.

"I felt like I was holding on to a rocket ship, and it looked great, sounded great. The story online that I shared [on] social media, the play-by-play was fancy," she admitted. Jet-setting across the world seems glamorous, but she was running on empty, averaging less than four hours of sleep at night.

It was no surprise, then, that she found herself standing in front of a departures board at JFK airport racking her brain trying to remember what city she was in and where she was supposed to be heading. That's not uncommon, especially for someone who had traveled on 210 flights in a single year. What happened next, though, changed her life.

To clear her head, she hurried over to the closest Starbucks to fill her tank, but when the barista rang her up, she froze. "I went to sign the receipt," she told me, "and I couldn't remember my name . . . I just stood there. It took me way too long to remember my name . . . it was the lowest low. And the tears [came]—not the hysterical ugly cry, but the what-have-I-done tears . . . I had created a situation where I was emotionally and physically bankrupt [even though] I was a millionaire."

Amy Jo hadn't forgotten something simple like her drink order; it wasn't like she had a little memory slip and couldn't recall where she had parked her car. She had worn herself out to a point where she literally couldn't remember her own name to sign the receipt in front of her.

When Amy Jo shared her story with me, there were long pauses and points where her voice gave in to the weight of her words. Here we are, years after this happened, but the emotional toll can still be felt—the reverberations of the choices she made, the life she had unknowingly created for herself.

You might recognize a piece of this story in your own life if you are striving to live in ways that look good to everyone else. Really, it's just perfectionism rearing its ugly head, spinning us in circles chasing after a result that can never be achieved. We wear ourselves out in the pursuit of perfection because it sounds good . . . and it looks good to everyone else.

Perfect is one of the biggest lies we tell ourselves.

SHINY OBJECT SYNDROME

There is no perfect, but we chase our tails trying to catch it, only to feel it slip through our grasp. We unknowingly use perfection as a tool to keep us from reaching our true potential. There are two kinds of perfectionists:

STRIVERS: The ones who start but set impossibly high standards. They set goals for themselves and work incredibly hard, but their

Perfect is one of the

BIGGEST
LIES

we tell *ourselves*.

standards are unreachable, so they are constantly battling against failure (a topic we will dive into later in chapter 7).

IDEALISTS: The ones who never start. They spend too much time imagining what the perfect future will look like and don't actually make the moves to begin. Because their idea is based on perfection, they know that they'll never achieve the grandiose vision they see in their mind. So they keep dreaming.

Idealists love to gather ideas like a squirrel, each one better than the last. Every shiny object distracts their attention, making them wonder which way to focus. The objects sparkle and gleam, blinding them from being able to see what direction they can move. They find themselves spinning in a circle moving from one idea to the next: spinning in place—not moving forward.

This Shiny Object Syndrome causes you to carry around idea debt for so long that the ideas begin to weigh on you. The unfinished ideas pull on you, and because they are ideas *not* in motion, you tend to over-romanticize them—they feel much more exciting than anything you are currently working on.

Perfectionism becomes a mask procrastination wears.

Like a squirrel decorating its den full of treasures—amassing a mountain of ideas without taking action—it's easy to get stuck in the thinking and planning phase and not move forward. It's a vicious cycle.

If you want to be great and do great things, you have to understand that the cost of greatness is commitment. Some of the best things in life start with a single step: making a choice. Committing to nothing just means you are distracted by everything.

But we use terms like *serial entrepreneur, Renaissance woman,* or *multipassionate* to describe ourselves, to justify not making a commitment.

THE MYTH OF THE MULTIPASSIONATE PERSON

Can you do me a favor? Can we agree to never use the term *multipassionate* again? Here's the reality: everyone is passionate about more than one thing. I can promise you that if you traveled the world far and wide, you would be hard pressed to find someone who says, "Yep. One thing. I only love one thing."

We *all* love lots of things!

Here's a little tough love: saying you're multipassionate is a cop-out to keep you from fully committing to anything.

Let that sink in. I know it's not easy to hear, but take a minute and pause. And then ask yourself, *Am I hiding behind an identity of being multipassionate so I don't have to really commit? So I don't have to choose?*

In my book *The Joy of Missing Out,* I shared the story of how I came to the realization that my first business did not fill my soul. It checked the boxes of paying the bills, feeding my kids, looking successful—it checked lots of boxes. Lots of practical boxes.

But there were quite a few unchecked. Felt fulfilling? No. Tied in with my natural gifts? Nope. Made me happy? Definitely not.

If you read chapter 2 of that book, you know that I did some deep work and found that there were three things that lit my fire: working with women, educating others, and productivity. It makes sense that I started my company, inkWELL Press Productivity Co., based on those three passions.

But here's what we didn't talk about in the book. There were more than three. You know why? Because I am multipassionate!* I want to stand John Cusack–style with my boombox raised above my head with Peter Gabriel blasting and proclaim my absolute love for multiple things: I'm a voracious bookworm, a cooking enthusiast, a wannabe baker, a carpenter-in-training, a lover of DIY renovations, an amateur designer—the list goes on and on. I'm guessing your list does too.

Here's an obvious question: Have you made a list? When you reflected back on your past, did you think about what it is you love and really take stock? Maybe that's the problem. If you think you are multipassionate, what is it you are passionate about? Or are you just hiding behind that word because you aren't really sure where to focus? Let's gain some clarity by doing a quick exercise that will help you home in on where you want to focus your energy. We do that by grabbing a piece of the pie:

<u>P</u>OWER • <u>I</u>MPACT • <u>E</u>XCITEMENT

You'll notice we are talking here about the head, the heart, and the gut—a lot like Enneagram—Powers (the head) + Impact (the heart) + Excitement (the gut). We need all three to be engaged because that's what is going to get us out of bed in the morning. It's what gets you to *want* to do the work instead of feeling like you *have* to do the work—even the not-so-glamorous parts of what you are passionate about.

And yes, there are not-so-glamorous parts to every job, every passion project, every task. Whoever it was that said "Love your job and you'll never work a day in your life" was a liar. We feel like if we are passionate about something, it should be easy. But doing what you love doesn't mean loving what you do every day.

Let me say that again for the people in the back: doing what you love doesn't mean loving what you do every day.

The word *passion* gets thrown around a lot, so we falsely believe that once we understand our passion, we are suddenly set for life. Now it should

---

* Oops. We agreed, didn't we? That we wouldn't use that word. Don't worry, I'll put a nickel in the ~~swear~~ multipassionate jar.

all become easy. There are going to be tough parts, parts we dread, and maybe even gross parts. (Passionate about animals? You know what I'm talking about here.) We're going to circle back on this idea later in the book, but I want us to acknowledge it now. Figuring out what you love doesn't suddenly make life a magic easy button.

But let's start with that first part—what is it you love? Choose to let go of the multipassionate identity by diving into what you really want. Let's grab that pie.

Step One: Get It Out of Your Head

To gain some clarity, start by making a list of the many things you feel passionate about—take out your overstuffed suitcase of things you love and unpack it. Just list it out. Don't worry about the order, don't worry about making it neat, just get them out of your head and onto a piece of paper in one nice, long column. If you downloaded the free reader's guide that comes with this book, I've already got a framework for you to use to help you list it all out. You can grab that in the Resources section of TanyaDalton.com.

Once you have your list out of your head and onto a sheet of paper, take a closer look. We want to assess our powers, impact, and excitement for each item on our lists. Let's go through each of those briefly.

Step Two: Powers

We hear the word *powers* and we think about Captain Marvel or the Bionic Woman. We believe that having powers means being superhuman, but if we take a good look, we'll realize we all have powers—dominant strengths that we are exceptionally good at. It's up to us to discover those powers and to use them for good. That's the hard part—not the using them for good, but the discovering them part. Because they are our natural powers, we tend to undervalue them; we think that since our gifts come naturally to us (because they are easy), they're *no big deal*.

My husband, John, is a perfect example of this. He can sit down, scratch a couple of quick pencil lines on a page, and suddenly he's drawn an incredible octopus or a bicycle. He's incredibly (infuriatingly) flippant about it. When people compliment his drawings, he shrugs them off and barely even acknowledges the praise. Finally exasperated one day, I asked him why. "Because it's not that hard—I just think about the shape, throw a few lines on the paper, and it's done. No big deal."

No big deal to him because it's a natural gift—a power. So that's where we start. What are the tasks, skills, and traits that come easy to you? What are the things that your friends, your family, and even your colleagues regularly compliment you on? It may be listening, writing, connecting people, encouraging others, organizing, cooking, using your intuition, analyzing, crunching numbers, planning, being creative, communicating . . . What are the things you do exceptionally well? This is not the time to be modest or shy away from your strengths. Own them.

You don't need to write them down; you already know deep inside what you are good at. Bring those gifts up to the surface and give them some air. Think about how these powers would work together to create synergy with the things you are passionate about. Give each of those passions you listed in step one a Power Score on a scale of 1 to 10.* How well does that passion fit in with your natural powers?

> **QUICK PEP TALK HERE:** Your powers don't have to limit you. Let's say you want to be a writer, but maybe spelling isn't a natural power for you. That's okay. Agatha Christie was a terrible speller and yet is still considered the world's best-selling novelist. Her gift for storytelling far outweighed her spelling struggles. Good editors can help with bad spelling—that's one of *their* powers.**
>
> Don't get discouraged, either, if people don't see eye-to-eye with you on your powers. Sometimes people shy away from things that are different from the status quo. Shakira, who is one of the top-selling recording artists in the world, was banned (yes, banned) from her childhood choir because of

---

* You may have multiple powers, but we only want to give one Power Score for each passion on your list. Think about how your powers work together. For example: love cooking, organizing, and socializing with people? That catering passion of yours should get a high Power Score of at least an 8!

** . . . and they can help with excessive use of commas, ellipses, and dashes. My editor loves me despite the fact that I toss around punctuation like beads during Mardi Gras . . . See what I mean?

her unique vibrato. Her dad told her to hold on to that unique sound because people would one day recognize her for it. Her "weakness" was really her strength. She didn't fit in; she actively stood out.

Step Three: Impact

There is a big difference between good work and great work. Good work means you are simply checking the boxes you need to get the job done. Great work, on the other hand, is the work that creates purpose and changes the world for you and for others.

If we want to live a life *On Purpose*, it means that we look beyond the checklist. We look for meaning within the daily steps so that we can feel fulfilled about the work we are creating and the impact it makes on the world.

In chapter 2 we started the conversation on impact. We discovered that we have the ability to touch the lives of about 80,000 people, so when we reframe how we look at our work and our passions, the question isn't "Will I make an impact?" It's "What kind of impact will I make?"

When we realize the actions we take make an impact, we can recognize that we are a catalyst for good in the world. We all have the ability to change—and improve—the world around us.

Being in the service of others doesn't necessarily mean charity work. It's the recognition that the work you do contributes to the greater good—and is a benefit to you and your life as well. This is when passion transforms and shifts into purpose. Passion is an internal flame that ignites you; purpose is how that flame ignites others as well.

How do you think committing to the passions you listed in step one will impact your life and the lives of others in a positive, meaningful way? Go through the list and give each one a rating from 1 to 10. Place this Impact Score next to the Power Score you did in the last step.

Step Four: Excitement

Listen, just because you are good at something doesn't mean you have to do it. I mean, I am good at math, but I'm not going to do my own accounting. I could, but I would *hate* it. I could also hang from my finger-nails for ten minutes if I had to, but that doesn't mean I should!

The problem is, it becomes this expectation: everyone assumes that you can (and should) just do the job because, well, you can. And it's flattering—it means you *are* good at what you do and that feels amazing. But it also makes it more difficult to say no, doesn't it? Allow me to lay a little truth on you here: just because you can, doesn't mean you should.

If these items on your list are things you are truly passionate about, then you need to have a genuine excitement for them. You can gauge your excitement by the gut feeling you get (just don't confuse nervousness with fear—nerves might just mean it's something new). You'll find that time seems to just disappear when you are in that rabbit hole working on a passion you have a true excitement for—big blocks of time just fly by. Or maybe you'll notice that you find yourself engaging in this passion without even thinking about it—like how John hangs up from his conference calls only to realize he's been doodling all over his notes.

Does the idea of taking on this project—this passion—really excite you? Then rate it as a 10. Feeling obligated to do it? That's a 1 on our scale. Place an Excitement Score next to your Impact Score for each item on that list.

Step Five: Add Them Up

Now that we have all of our pieces of pie lined up, it's time to add them and get a total for each item on your list. Yes, I purposely neglected to mention that math is a part of this process, but I promise, it's easy. Simply add your three scores—Power Score + Impact Score + Excitement Score—to get your final tally for each passion. With those numbers you can now rank your passions from highest to lowest—and now we've got some clarity on how you want to move forward. Easy as pie, right?

Taking a good, hard look at all of your passions truly will help give some clarity about where you want to focus. Here's something to remember though: you are expected to love more than one thing. Deciding to focus doesn't mean you toss aside everything else you love.

Back when I took some time to figure out what I wanted to do for my career, when I decided to open inkWELL Press, I did have a lot of other passions on that list. But I knew I couldn't make them the focus *and* go after my dream.

I never let go of my love for the other things on that list. One of the big ones? Building. I love using power tools and creating something new with my own two hands. I knew I didn't want to make that my primary focus, but I also knew I needed to find a way to bring that into my life.

Every year for my birthday, I give myself a gift: time and space to build. I spend a few weeks planning, measuring, and sketching, and then I pull out all my tools and build something from scratch. I've built a bed, a set of outdoor couches, a desk—every year it's something different. I get the kids and John involved, and we make a long weekend of it. It's something I look forward to every single year.

You can be passionate about a lot of things, but you have to choose to focus on the passions that are the most important *to you*.

IS THE GRASS GREENER?

So often we give in to the Shiny Object Syndrome because we are so busy trying to do what *everybody* else is doing that we lose sight of our own unique strengths that make *us* great. We falsely believe that there is some sort of secret formula for success, so we look around and see what everyone else is doing and we think we need to be doing that same thing too.

We assume we need to have the exact same skills, the exact same drive and passion they do, in order to be successful. We get caught in the comparison trap where we are struggling to fit in and keep up with everyone else. All while losing sight of who we are at our core.

That's why it's sometimes hard to see our own powers—we discount them because they don't look the same as everyone else's. So we try and fit in, mimicking what we see others doing because we want to be successful too.

It's important to remember that when we see others being successful, it's not because they're following along to the beat of someone else's drum. They're using their own unique gifts in ways that bring them success. That's the key takeaway here. We have to remember that there's more than one path to success—you need to blaze your own trail.

Want in on a secret? The grass is greener on the other side because it's fertilized with bullshit. What we see on the tiny little screens of our phones is not the full story—we can't see what's pushed to the outside edges of those images.

It's easy to assume that those people we see have it all together. This is an illusion we've created for ourselves and, in reality, the most impressive people have had large setbacks, changes in direction, and many moments of doubt.

There are no overnight success stories . . . unless they stayed up all night working. Overnight success is one of those bedtime stories we tell ourselves because it happens to other people. But it doesn't really. We just don't peek behind the curtains and see that they've been sweating away all along. It takes a lot of exertion, work, and stress to make your jam-packed social media life look effortless.

LET'S WATER YOUR GRASS

We always worry that we are getting the short end of that stick. It's true. Have you ever noticed that whatever line you choose at the grocery store, it's the slowest? Or when you change lanes during a traffic jam, yours seems to be the only one at a standstill? You aren't alone in feeling that way—funny enough, all the drivers in all the other lanes feel exactly the same. We all falsely believe that somehow everyone else is moving along much faster and easier than we are.

This is why even though that one ridiculously long security line at the airport may seem senseless, it's actually done by design. It's been proven that a single queue alleviates stress because it increases the feeling of *fairness*. Aviation management expert Julian Lukaszewicz shared, "If you implement a one-queue system for check-in, or for security . . . [where] you go just to the next available counter, passengers perceive it as more fair because each person is standing in the same line. It's strange but true because you always think the queue next to you moves quicker."

I find this research fascinating because it proves that we are constantly scanning, looking around to make sure everything is doled out evenly; we desperately want life to be fair. But when we do this, we are losing time up on our tiptoes peering enviously over that fence. We need to choose, instead, to focus our time and energy on what we can do. It's good to know what others are doing, but if it's driving our motivation, we will always feel that we've fallen short.

Stop worrying about how much greener it is on the other side of the fence and choose to water your own grass. Your grass has the ability to be lush and green, but it has to be tended and nurtured. One way to do that is to transform the comparison game into a springboard. What we admire (or even envy) is what we want to embody in our own lives, so let's take some time to reflect and understand why.

Use the Fifth Why method to get to the heart of what it is you admire about these people. Oftentimes, it's not the people themselves but the qualities they embody that we envy. I've given you a set of questions to get you started, and I've added a few subquestions to help you dive deeper:

1. What is it that I admire about them?
   - Is it superficial or do I genuinely respect them?
   - Do I have any similar qualities?
2. What is it that they have that I wish I had?
   - Is that something I really want, or is it something I think I am supposed to want?
   - Would I really be happy if I had those things?
3. How does this fit into my values?
   - Where do my values differ from theirs?
   - How could I express more of the values I admire?

4. What have they realistically done to get where they are today?
   - How might my path be similar or different?
   - What am I willing to do to get to that same place?

Take what you've learned here to move you forward to whatever it is *you* really do want. Let's shift from looking at others to looking at ourselves and what we can do to find success in our own lives.

WHAT IS SUCCESS?

I think we can all agree that success is what we are striving for. When the average person is asked what they want most in life, success (without question) will be listed somewhere in their top three. But if we love the idea of success, don't we need to define what success really means? And why we want to pursue it?

We are wearing ourselves out, trying our hardest to live up to false standards, playing by these arbitrary rules and fitting into tight little boxes in order to become successful. We've become a society obsessed with success and all that it entails.

In fact, 14 percent of elite athletes would willingly accept a fatal heart condition if it meant they could win an Olympic gold medal. To them, death apparently feels like a fair price to pay for a fleeting, glorious moment of success.

Maybe you can see the high cost of chasing success in your own life:

It's in the long hours you work that have caused you to put off your date night for the third time in a row.

They know how work is just slammed right now, don't they?

Perhaps it's hidden within the back-to-back meetings that compel you to bail on lunch with your friends (again).

There's just never a good time to get together. There's just not room in my schedule for things like that anymore.

Or maybe you can see it in the number of times you've justified big chunks of time away from your family because you'll make it up to them once you get that promotion (or land the account or close the sale or whatever it is you are chasing after).

I'm doing this for us and our future; surely they understand that I'll have more time later.

We are stretching and straining to achieve success no matter the cost. But because we've never taken the time to really create a definition of what success looks like, it becomes a finish line we can never reach. Which means we are constantly striving for it with no way of knowing how we are actually doing. So we look around in an effort to measure our success and gauge where we are by looking at the competition. We look around and ask not *How am I doing?* but *How am I doing compared to everyone else?*

We are craning our necks, watching what everyone else is doing, and we worry we need to do more. Brooke Harrington, a professor at the Copenhagen Business School, has discovered that rich people—who, by most standards, have achieved a high bar of success—still worry about having *enough*.

She explained, "The sensation of 'being well-off' is not about fulfilling a childhood dream of buying a sailboat or something; feeling wealthy is about comparison with others in your reference group. So the question is not what individuals want to buy, but what they feel they must buy in order to keep up their status."

There's that word *enough* again. We talked about it back in chapter 2, and yet it keeps coming back like a boomerang aimed for our heads. When will enough actually be enough? Comparing ourselves to others becomes our measuring stick of success, and if that stick shows that we are falling short, we find ourselves hustling, grinding, and sacrificing everything to achieve the mirage of success . . . everything that's really important, that is.

Success itself isn't bad, but when success is hinged on what everyone else is doing, that's when we begin to lose our focus on what we really want. That's when we feel like we need to say yes to anything and everything and when we begin to believe that we need more simply because that's what everyone else is doing.

We need to redefine what success looks like to us.

SUCCESS ON YOUR OWN TERMS

"When you're in those deep trenches and you've built something that the world says is a success, it's really hard to break those walls of pride down." Those wise words were shared with me by my friend Kristen Ley, founder of Thimblepress.

To the outside world, Kristen had the ultimate success—a thriving business with products on the shelves of over 1,500 retailers, including Target and Nordstrom; a big team; two huge buildings; and a storefront downtown. As she put it, "We were growing and becoming what everyone in the world defines as a success." But behind the scenes she wasn't just burning the candle at both ends; her candle was an inferno.

Sure, the tiny little squares on her social media feed exuded success, but that's a highlight reel. There's a lot of work that goes into making life look easy all the time, and when you're constantly striving to keep up with what everyone expects, it's exhausting.

"For a long time, I was living for someone else's version of success and I wasn't living for my own. . . . I was putting my stock into what everyone else thought of me and . . . wanted for me." That meant saying yes to a million little things; it meant running herself ragged chasing busy and showing up for everyone else in her life except herself.

"You can do everything you want in life . . . you just can't do it all at once, and that's what I had to realize," Kristen confided in me. She needed to get back to her *why*—her purpose. Her company was built to help people experience more joy through celebrating their everyday lives, but Kristen wasn't feeling any of that joy. She needed to choose to focus in on the things that really supported her purpose and infused more happiness into her own life.

"I had to let go of some things that maybe I thought I wanted, but didn't need . . . and I analyzed, 'What do we do our best at? What's our winners?' We need[ed] to get rid of the things that aren't serving people well." It's now been several years since Kristen redefined success as not just bringing joy to her customers, but also to her own life.

Failing to focus is one of the biggest stumbling blocks I see with the women I coach. We want to do it all in the relentless pursuit of success. But we can't. Let me rephrase that: when we try to do everything, we end up doing nothing very well. We'll feel burned out, unsatisfied, and exhausted.

Instead of spreading ourselves thin and saying yes to twenty things and doing them halfway, let's say yes to five and do them *extraordinarily* well. Let's pour ourselves fully, completely, and wholly into what we offer to the world.

CAN YOU SIGN YOUR NAME?

My kids come to me from time to time to share something they've created or achieved. I can see them looking at me, their eyes silently asking for a gold star of approval. When this happens, I'll ask Jack and Kate: "Can you sign your name to it?" Meaning, whatever it is you have done, are you willing to place your signature in the corner like it's a work of art?

I don't want them seeking my approval; they don't need it. I want them to discover the satisfaction that can be found in ourselves when we approve of the work we've done. *Anything worth doing is worth doing well.* That's the phrase uttered a million times at my house to my kids—*anything*, by the way, includes how we interact in our relationships, how we pursue our hobbies, and even how we do our chores. Let's find that sense of satisfaction of a job well done.

When we choose to focus and when we give ourselves to fewer things, we are able to give our best selves. Let's go through life feeling like it's a precious work of art and then choose to sign our name on it.

What if we made the choice to commit to focus in on fewer, more important things? What if we let go of the pursuit of absolute perfection and allowed ourselves to be real and honest? What if we decided to stop craning our necks looking left and right and every which way, trying to keep up with what we think we are *supposed* to do? What if we chose to see the gifts we have been given in our lives? What if we used them as springboards to drive us forward and give us the momentum we need to look toward the future?

That's where we are going next.

five

CHOOSE TO MAKE A PLAN

"Are you B to Y?"

I had just plopped into a chair to get my hair and makeup done before heading on stage to speak to a room full of businesswomen. It had been a rough trip—my flight had been delayed hour after hour, and I'd ended up having to fly cross-country on a 4:00 a.m. flight. Nevertheless, I was fired up about getting out there and talking with women about growing their companies. Speaking at events is one of my very favorite parts of my purpose because it combines one of my superpowers, speaking, with my love for connecting with women. Getting my hair and makeup done after a long night of travel felt like the cherry on top of an already amazing day in the making.

While she combed her fingers through my hair, Noel Sweeny had smiled and asked me about my job. I had given her the short version—the one I use at cocktail parties or when meeting new people for the first time. "I am redefining productivity for women," I said. "To help them understand that it's not about doing more, it's doing what's most important. I give them the tools and training to help them confidently step into intentional leadership."

Her eyes lit up and then a serious shadow quickly passed over her face as she lowered her chin to look at me in the mirror, eye to eye. Then came that confusing question: "So, are you B to Y?"

To say I was thoroughly confused would be an understatement. I wondered if this was some phrase used in the styling industry or some new business terminology I'd never heard, or if it was just the time-zone difference that made my brain unable to compute what she was asking.

I think I must have looked a little dazed because she waved her hands as she laughed and said, "I'm just wondering if you're B to Y because that's where I struggle. I know where I am and I know where I want to go, but I have no idea how to get there. I've got the A to Z down. It's the B to Y that's tripping me up. I don't know the steps in-between to get me there."

B to Y . . . the steps needed to get you from A to Z. It made perfect sense—even to someone who had slept in an airport the night before.

Noel shared with me her big purpose in life—to help people with their appearance so they can better connect with their audience, allowing them to spread their message. She told me that she believes hair and makeup is a catalyst to reach people and to help them find out who they really are. Wow. That's a purpose statement right there. Big and bold and impactful. So much bigger than focusing on the job of being a styling expert. Noel has a much bigger calling—a larger vision she is working toward. I love that.

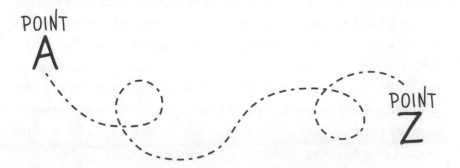

So, she knows where she's starting (point A) and where she wants to go (point Z), but what's the path that will get her there? She told me, "I get excited . . . but then I get stuck on how to get there. It can feel heavy and overwhelming."

Maybe you've felt this way—that you have a great idea or a big vision of what you want, but there are so many possibilities, you have no idea of how to really start.

Noel explained it in a way that really connected me with how she was struggling. She said, "At least when you have your kids, you have a loose eighteen-year plan. It's not a perfect plan, but at least it gives you a path—at this time they'll be talking, and here they'll be walking. Here's when they'll start school, and so on. It's not exactly the same for everyone, but at least there are some markers to see where you are." In business and in life there's no map, so we can easily get lost or frustrated. We get caught up in false metrics, paying attention to where other people are in their own journey and where we assume we should be.

If you read *The Joy of Missing Out* or if you've listened to my podcast, you know one of my key phrases: Overwhelm isn't having too much to do. It's not knowing where to start.

Right there, my new friend Noel had touched on exactly that. *We have no idea of how to really start.* No wonder she felt overwhelmed. We need to create a map for ourselves.

As Noel mentioned, a map doesn't need to be perfect. It doesn't have to tell us exactly when or where each step will happen, but it does create landmarks to help us keep to our path. Markers help us stay the course.

FINDING OUR WAY

Here's a fascinating fact I learned when diving into this idea: researchers have found that if you are lost in a place where there are no landmarks—like a forest or a desert—you will find yourself wandering in circles rather than making a straight path to safety. They discovered that walking in circles is the result of "increasing uncertainty about where straight ahead is." With no clear landmarks, we will continuously make microadjustments to what we *perceive* as straight.

We believe we are staying true to the path we want, but without guidance we are spiraling off track. In fact, the group leader for the study discovered that "even though people may be convinced they are walking in a straight line, their perception is not always reliable."

We need clear guideposts to truly move forward in the direction we want. Having these landmarks gives us the confidence to understand where we are, where we are going, and how to reroute when obstacles detour us off our path—and yes, there will be obstacles even when we have a plan!

Think about it: If you decided you wanted to drive across the country from San Francisco, California, to Orlando, Florida, and you did it with no map, no compass, and no landmarks to guide you, would you really make it to the front gates of Disney World?

I can tell you right now, with absolute certainty, I would not. I could end up in Central America or—let's be really honest here—I might find myself up in Canada. I have a terrible sense of direction (definitely not one of my superpowers).

But even if you happen to be able to tell your east from your west simply by how the moss grows on trees, without a map it would probably take you two or three times longer to FastPass your way onto Space Mountain—or you might end up in Tampa. Yes, that's not far off the target, but wear your mouse ears there and they may call an exterminator.

We need to know what roads to take, where to turn, and what's coming up ahead, but how do we create a route to get us from A to Z when there's no map?

We'll have to create our own.

This is no different from the ancient practice of wayfinding. For centuries before the invention of the compass or GPS, Pacific Islanders navigated across the vast, open ocean using the stars, the sun, and other landmarks for guidance. Wayfinding is essentially the process of orienting yourself when traveling over unknown paths.

Just as Noel mentioned, life doesn't come with an instruction booklet.

There are no marked trails for us to follow—it's up to us to blaze them ourselves. We have the ability to design our own map to get us to where we want to go, but when we don't have any bearings of where we are and there are no landmarks around, it can be frustrating.

ARE WE THERE YET?

If you've ever traveled with kids on a long car trip, you've heard that question asked more than five million times.* I may be underestimating here, but as someone who's been in a car for fourteen hours straight with two small kids, that sounds about right to me.

The problem was, I began to realize, my kids had no concept of where we were on our journey. They felt disoriented because they had no bearings as to how we were progressing toward our destination. It's no wonder they were so restless and irritated! I came up with an idea to help them do their own version of wayfinding during a summer road trip from Dallas to Denver.

Using the two handles attached to the ceiling of the car, I ran a piece of string from the driver's side across to the passenger's side. On the driver's side, I placed a small piece of paper with a picture of our house and the word "HOME" underneath, and then I placed a clothespin next to it.

Next I set up a series of little tags across the string: some had the names of the cities we would drive through; others had images I'd printed out from the internet of the different sights we'd see, like Cadillac Ranch in Amarillo; on another, there was a drawing of a pool and the name of the hotel we'd be staying at on the border of New Mexico. There were probably ten to twelve tags all told, lined up along that string. And each time we reached a new landmark on our trip, the kids would cheer and celebrate and move the clothespin over to the next tag.

---

* Or . . . a short car trip . . . or a medium car trip . . . or any car trip whatsoever . . .

Slowly that clothespin made its way from the driver's seat all the way across the car to the other side. What's funny, though, is that the trip didn't seem slow at all. It seemed fun. It made for some great car games because the kids would start noticing signs for the next landmark. They'd count down the miles, getting giddy with excitement as the numbers dwindled down and we got closer.

But here was the real bonus: they stopped asking (or, let's be honest, complaining) about how much longer we'd be in the car because they could physically see our progress on the string. They knew when we were halfway there, they knew when we were one city away, and they could see exactly where they were on the journey.

Here's the big question for us: Where are we going on our trips around the sun? Do you know? Do you see the progress, or do you feel disoriented—unsure of where exactly you are and what you need to do next?

Ultimately, the destination we are all trying to get to is our Cathedral, right? That big purpose we talked about in the last chapter—the big vision we are living toward.*

You'll remember we agreed that Cathedral Thinking is dreaming, planning, and creating blueprints that reach far into the future. In chapter 4 we dreamed of what that towering Cathedral might look like, and now it's time for us to put some plans in place.

But when we have a big Cathedral that seems far away, it's no surprise that we all feel like my kids did in the car traveling cross-country—irritable, frustrated, and out of control. Are we there yet? Why does it seem like we aren't moving any closer?!

We need to design our own route and we'll use wayfinding to help us. Sounds easy enough, but when we go to put pen to paper, it can feel overwhelming. Where do we even begin? How do you know your landmarks? I've got an easy exercise to help break it down so you can see your potential, what's possible, and what's really practical.

---

* Notice I didn't say *working* toward.

POTENTIAL, POSSIBLE, AND PRACTICAL

Let's think of our path to our Cathedral like a map:

RIGHT
NOW

YOUR
POTENTIAL

This is your potential—if there was nothing holding you back and you were free to make the impact you wanted, what would your Cathedral look like in ten or twenty years? In the last chapter, we did an activity to help you see your strongest passions. Use what you learned as a springboard for dreaming about what that could look like even further into the future. Write down your big dream at the end of your timeline.

Now, let's think about what's possible. That Cathedral off in the distance looks really far away, so let's back up our timeline a bit. If you know your potential, let's figure out what's really possible in the next three to five years. What do you think you could accomplish in that time that will get you a little bit closer to your Cathedral? Let's write that down—it's a landmark on our path.

RIGHT
NOW

POSSIBLE:
3-5 YEARS

YOUR
POTENTIAL

It still feels pretty far off, though, doesn't it? Your future self five years down the road is going to feel like a stranger right now, but that's okay because we are going to keep breaking this down bit by bit. Now that we see what's possible, let's discover what's practical. What is feasible for you to accomplish in the next twelve to eighteen months? Don't just think about it—brainstorm, dream big, think about what is truly achievable, and then write this down as your Practical Landmark.

RIGHT   PRACTICAL: POSSIBLE: YOUR
NOW   12–18 MONTHS   3–5 YEARS   POTENTIAL

Okay, this feels more attainable, doesn't it? It may not feel easy, but it should feel like it's something you can definitely accomplish within the next year or so.

NOW LET'S PRIORITIZE

We can clearly see those big Potential, Possible, and Practical Landmarks off in the distance on our timeline, which will help us in our wayfinding. We see what's practical in twelve months, but can we break that down even more? What do you think you can accomplish in the shorter term? Maybe in three, six, or nine months? These are now your Priority Landmarks— the tasks, projects, and objectives you want to prioritize right now to get you moving on your path toward your Cathedral. We really should call those Priority Landmarks what they are—goals.

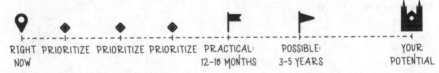

RIGHT PRIORITIZE PRIORITIZE PRIORITIZE PRACTICAL: POSSIBLE: YOUR
NOW   12–18 MONTHS   3–5 YEARS   POTENTIAL

With an *On Purpose* life, we aren't just setting goals; we are creating our own path to get us to that higher purpose. Goals are simply the landmarks to help keep you from wandering in circles. Goals are not the end point but the guideposts to help keep you moving toward your Cathedral.

Most people look at goal setting in a vacuum. They set their goals willy-nilly based on what they think they are *supposed* to be doing. They look around and think: *I should probably do X . . . I don't really know why or how, but everyone else is doing it, so I should too.* There's no path in mind, there's no bigger vision. Each goal is set because we randomly decide we *should* be doing something.

We have to stop *shoulding* on ourselves because when we follow what we think we are supposed to do instead of following what we feel excited to do, we lose our passion for life. It's no surprise we feel uninspired and burned out.

In fact, 81 percent of people fail to follow through on their resolutions and goals, with a staggering 23 percent drop-off in the first week alone. Why is that, you might ask? Because most people don't tie their goals to a bigger vision—they don't take the time to ask the fearless question: *Why?*

Why am I thinking about doing this? Why do I think this will improve my life? Why do I want to do this at all?

Here's a bold statement: If the goals you set don't have a long-term benefit, then they're not worth your time. If you are looking for the quick win, you'll get that winning feeling and then it will quickly disappear, leaving you jonesing for that high. This is referred to as the goal-setting paradox—a very real, very measurable drop in life satisfaction after a goal is achieved.

Yes, there's the initial high when crossing the finish line, but it's followed with a feeling of *Now what?*, which can sink into a real negative space. We can combat that, though, by linking our goals to a bigger objective—our Cathedral. When we link our actions to a higher purpose, our satisfaction increases as we achieve each goal because we know we are making progress.

When goals are tied to something we really want—when they are tied to the vision of where it is we want to go in life, they aren't just goals—they are fresh landmarks helping us make our way to our Cathedral.

Let me give you a few examples of what a wayfinding map could look like. Why don't we start with a really impressive real-life Cathedral—one that we touched on in the last chapter—the race to put a man on the moon.

PRIMATE IN SPACE / FARSIDE OF MOON / LAUNCH SATELLITE / CREATE NAV SYSTEM / SPACE WALK / MAN ON THE MOON

You can see that when we start with just focusing on the smallest step, we can get to the "one giant leap." Even gigantic, awe-inspiring Cathedrals can be accomplished when we break them down. Truthfully, though, that Race-to-the-Moon Cathedral is a lot bigger than most of us will have, so let's float back down to Earth and look at some other examples:

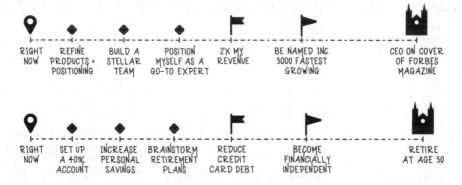

GOALS WITH IMPACT

Goal setting seems like a simple concept, so we think it should be easy, which is why we feel like failures when our goals don't really work out. I'm always surprised to find that so many people don't have a framework for creating their goals. They think that if they state them out loud, somehow the universe will make it all happen. (That's not how manifesting works either, no matter what some popular social media influencers say.) Like anything in this world, if it's worthwhile, it's going to take some work, and it's going to require some planning.

For years I have talked about setting SMART goals, a method that's been around since 1981. SMART goals provide a clear and simple framework for defining your goals, plus the acronym works really well to make it simple to remember and use—no tools needed. There's a reason why, decades later, people still use it.

But when I taught my clients about the framework, I was always needing to modify it and adjust it to really work in our modern world. A lot has changed since 1981, and it's time for an upgrade. Using the SMART system as a model, I wanted to create a simple framework to act as an update to help us define our goals.

The IMPACT goals framework follows the model of being simple to use and requires no tools:

I NSPIRATIONAL

M EASURABLE

P URPOSE-DRIVEN

A DAPTABLE

C HALLENGING

T IMED

Using the IMPACT system, you will find that defining and understanding your goals becomes easier. We want to create goals for ourselves that are aligned with a bigger cause or purpose, but we also want to make sure they are achievable. This simple framework will help with that.

Before we dive into each of the letters of IMPACT, I want to mention something: this framework is for projection, to help us understand and write out exactly what we want for our goals. This isn't the *how* but the *what* of goal setting—what is it you are wanting to accomplish? We'll talk about how we'll achieve these goals in the next section of the book, but first, let's focus in on what you want to achieve.

CHOOSE YOUR OWN ADVENTURE

Here's something you may have forgotten: life is a choose-your-own-adventure. You get to be the one who chooses the goals you set, and you also get to choose how deep you go down the rabbit hole. After working with thousands of women in all walks of life, I know it's important to dive into some of the granular details of how to really set your goals.

I know this because I've watched way too many of these amazing women struggle and then question their self-worth because they didn't set goals in a way that truly set them up for success. I am about to dive into each of the letters so that you can feel empowered to set your own goals. I promise to keep it easy, but I also realize that, for some of you, this may feel like too many details right now. You may feel like you'd rather revisit this section after making it through the rest of the book.

My editor and I discussed putting some of these details in an appendix, but you and I both know, no one reads those back pages! They're like the punch bowl wedding present your great-aunt bought for you that sits gathering dust in a hard-to-reach cabinet. I want to put the information here where you can easily reference it when you are ready. That might be right now or it might be in a few weeks.

Ready to choose?

a. I feel ready to set some goals! *Read on, my friend.*
b. I want to come back to this later. *Let's meet back up on page 101.*

IMPACT GOAL FRAMEWORK

Inspirational

Your goals need to be exciting. You have to be fired up to do the work, so make your goals inspirational. Remember, your words matter—and they matter more than ever when it comes to setting your goals.

You want to make your goal attractive, so focus on the positive aspect. It's not the dread of sitting in a chair typing out a lot of words that will motivate you; it's the joy of hearing from the readers affected by your writing. It's not the skipping of dessert; it's the confidence of feeling healthy.

Write your goals out in a positive statement, as if it's an inevitable outcome. After all, when you go to dinner and order your food, you don't tell the waiter all the foods you don't want. You focus on what you want to see on that plate in front of you. We want to do that with our goals—we want to focus on the good we want to see. For example, it's not that we want to stop smoking; it's that we want to be a nonsmoker. Start identifying yourself that way using your words.

Here's the catch, though: we need to make sure we are inspirational but also realistic. No matter what we decide we want to pursue, we have to consider that there will be times of sunshine and times of torrential rain.

In other words, are we willing to fight for this future even when things are tough? We don't want to just be in love with the result—the end point of that future—we need to love the messy in-between parts too.

If the idea of struggling quite a bit to get there doesn't appeal, it's okay to let the dream go. Perhaps it's not really your dream after all. There's something else out there. You just need to keep looking or shift how that future looks to suit whatever it is you really do want.

A few years ago I was speaking at an event and, during cocktail hour, I was lucky enough to chat with a woman named Lisa. She confided in me that one of her goals was to travel across the country running her business out of an RV with her family in tow. She loved the idea of the open roads and the freedom to explore while growing her business.

For years she had dreamed of this lifestyle. She romanticized it and imagined all the fun she would have with her family . . . and then she met Susan, who had lived that lifestyle for an entire year. Susan had loved her RV experience and eagerly shared all the logistics of planning, homeschooling, and work-life on the road. She bubbled over with excitement and couldn't wait to do it again.

You would assume this fired up Lisa about her own trip, but it did just the opposite. Hearing Susan run through all the ins and outs of life on the road, Lisa realized she was in love with the idea, but not the actual day-in-day-out logistics. You could say she was in love with the destination but not the journey itself.* She was at a crossroads, so she needed to make a choice: kill the dream or shift it to fit what she really wanted.

Lisa chose to adjust her dream, and she now travels each year with her family for two weeks in an RV. Even with making this tweak, they will still travel to all fifty states before her kids leave for college. Her dream was never really about being on the road for long stretches; it was really about spending time with her kids, deepening their relationships by exploring the country together.

---

* Alanis Morissette would say, "And isn't it ironic? Don't you think?"

Taking the time to really decide what she wanted out of her goal has made a huge difference for Lisa. Her dream shift has helped her feel more content with her current life and has made it possible to actually achieve what she really wants—*time spent traveling together as a family.*

Measurable

We don't want to make measurement our prime focus, but we do need to see we've made headway. It's satisfying to see how far we've come, and often when we don't see progress, we feel discouraged. When climbing the steep hills of a goal, there will be days when our legs feel like they may give way and we need to catch our breath.

We can look behind us and see how far we've already come—there's power in measuring our progress.

This means we need to talk about numbers. I realize that for someone who has admitted several times (in this book alone) that I hate math, I have talked about it quite a bit, haven't I? But numbers are important—especially when it comes to making goals measurable. So let's talk about the two most common types of numbers when it comes to goals:

- **FREQUENCY NUMBERS**: a pattern of occurrences or the number of times we regularly notice ourselves behaving a certain way.
  Example: I will ride my bike three times a week.

- **QUANTITY NUMBERS**: numbers that we add up over time—they accumulate and grow.
  Example: I will ride my bike thirty miles a week.

What I've noticed is, we seem to have a bad habit of using those numbers to decide our value and worth. Remember this: You are more than a number. Whether that's the number on a scale, the number of followers you have on social media, or the number you bring home on your paycheck. Numbers do not define you, and they do not determine your worth.

Often, quantity numbers become our default when it comes to our goals. For example, when we think about getting healthy, we immediately zoom in and look at the digits on the scale and declare that we need to lose ten pounds.

But if your Cathedral includes living a healthy lifestyle that allows you to be active well into your golden years, then is that ten pounds really the goal? Or would it be better to track the habit of healthy eating or working out or even meal planning to help you stop swinging by the fast-food joint around the corner for dinner? Quantity numbers often focus on the short-term win, not the long term. Your mom was right: it's always quality over quantity.

If this is the case, how do we track something abstract, like healthy eating or meal planning?

Let's choose to focus on the momentum, not just the measurement. A habit tracker is a great way to see that forward motion. It's just like that clothespin making its way across the car for my kids—it will give you a solid understanding of your progress and bring you satisfaction because you'll see the progress.

You'll notice that this strategy doesn't have a quantifiable number attached to it at all—it's simply the act of watching the clothespin move across the car that showed the progress. It's the same little hit of dopamine your brain gets when you cross something off your list—it feels good. You can even use a color-coding system on your habit tracker: green for days that went incredibly well, yellow for days where you feel you did pretty well, and blue for days that just don't seem to be on track at all.* (We all have those days and it's okay!)

When you start to see a strong pattern of green day after day, don't you think you'll be more likely to keep up that pattern? You know we love patterns, so let's use that to our advantage. Before you know it, you've cultivated a healthy habit that allows for the progress to carry on and continue long after the "official goal" has been reached—that's when goal setting begins to shift and transform into living with intention.

Purpose-Driven

Listen, if you are five chapters deep in this book and you are surprised to find that your goals need to be tied to your purpose, you may need to close the cover and

---

* Don't we all just want to avoid the red pen? Brings me flashbacks of high school calculus homework. No thank you.

head back to page 1. You and I both know that we need to tie our goals into something meaningful—something bigger than just reaching the finish line.

You'll remember we've talked about the idea that doing what you love doesn't mean loving what you do every day. There will be rough patches on the way to any goal. Life is never easy, but if you can connect your goal to something you truly care about, it will make the task easier.

When I work directly with entrepreneurs, helping them align their businesses with their purpose, we talk about the fact that we are not selling products or services, but solving problems for our customers. When you take the attention away from the "thing you sell" and focus instead on the larger, bigger impact of what you create through your offerings, it completely shifts your mindset and allows you to do better.

This is no different than how our friend Noel, at the start of this chapter, sees herself not as a stylist but as someone helping to empower women with confidence. She's connected her daily work to a much larger, more impactful purpose. She's not applying fake lashes and lipstick; she's arming women with the confidence to raise their voices and spread their messages.

You don't have to be curing cancer to have a worthwhile cause or purpose, but you can choose to see what you do and what you are pursuing as part of a bigger plan.

In fact, one Yale University study found that janitors working in hospitals who think of their work not just as mopping up messes but instead as a part of the healing process, are significantly more satisfied and more motivated to do their work. There's that word again—*satisfaction*. It doesn't matter if you are mopping up vomit in a hospital or washing dishes in the back of a restaurant; being satisfied isn't tied to a number or your title. It's tied to seeing the bigger value in the work you do.

In the study, the custodians who didn't see themselves as janitors chose to describe their job as being "an ambassador for the hospital." One even called herself a healer because she "creates[s] sterile spaces in the hospital. [Her] role . . . is to do everything [she] can to promote the healing of the patients."

Tie your goals to a bigger purpose and you will feel more satisfied too.

ADAPTABLE AND CHALLENGING

These next two components of an IMPACT goal need to be discussed together because they go hand in hand. We want to make sure the goals we are working toward challenge us. This journey to achieve our own zone of greatness will require us to step outside of our zone of comfort. Our comfort zone is a dangerous place to live because as much as we seem to enjoy comfort and routine, we are often happiest when challenged and making progress. If our goals are too easy or we don't feel that we have to work hard to achieve them, we tend to lose motivation and get bored.

One of my favorite studies that illustrates this idea was done by Carol Dweck. She took a group of students and presented them with a series of complex puzzles. After completing the puzzles, all the subjects were told that they did well, but one group was recognized for working hard while another group was acknowledged as being naturally smart. Students were then allowed to choose from a new set of puzzles, which ranged from easy to difficult.

Here's where it gets interesting: the "smart puzzlers" chose the easiest puzzle, while the "hard-working puzzlers" chose the most complex puzzle. Because they were complimented on something that they *do* have control over—like choosing to challenge themselves—they performed better and approached new challenges with a more optimistic attitude.

When we feel empowered to overcome challenges, we become unstoppable. What I love about this research is it proves that when we create positive bread-crumbs for ourselves, we'll continue the pattern. And it goes to show—your words matter.* Set a challenging goal and you will more than likely be optimistic and motivated to keep growing outside of your comfort zone.

Here's the caveat, though. We don't want to set goals that are so challeng-ing that we feel like we are constantly battling to keep our heads just above the quicksand. We need to allow for some adaptability because life demands it.

If we allow a little more grace and breathing room with our goals, we'll find that motivation follows. We're bound to have some days that don't go well, and if we immediately look at those days as a failure, it becomes easy to quit. We've all heard the Jeff Bezos quote about Amazon: "We are stubborn on vision. We are flexible on details." Flexibility gives us that grace we need.

---

* One of my own personal takeaways from this study was that I stopped praising my kids and my team at work for being naturally gifted or simply "good" at what they do. I now focus my compliments more on their effort and have seen them flourish because of that small switch.

Goals are not a pass-fail class in college. We need to allow for a little bit of grace for ourselves because there are weeks when we are going to kill it with these goals. There are weeks when we are not, and that's okay because every day is different.

There are two ways we can make sure that we're challenging ourselves while also being adaptable:

AVERAGE: Use the word *average* when talking about your measurement.
- **Example:** I will save an average of $100 each month.
- **Why this works:** Using the word *average* allows you to possibly save more in certain months and, in tougher months, save a bit less; it all evens out.

MTO METHOD: Set a Minimum, a Target, and an Outrageous measurement for yourself.
- **Example:** Each month I will save a minimum of $75, but I will target saving $100. If possible, I will save the outrageous amount of $150 dollars.
- **Why this works:** With the example above, at a minimum, if you save $75, you've met that goal. But really, you're shooting for $100, while $150 is your stretch goal. It is nice to have a stretch goal, because it can push you, in those months where things are going pretty well, to go a little bit further.

Both of these methods work really well in encouraging you to push yourself to reach a little bit higher and challenge yourself while still keeping your feet firmly on the ground in reality. Life works so much better when we allow room for a little grace for ourselves—just because an accomplishment is challenging doesn't mean it can't be enjoyable. Having flexibility allows for that.

TIMED

Without deadlines in place, we'll find that we constantly put our dreams on a shelf for Someday. *Someday*, you whisper to yourself, *when the kids get older or when I have enough money or when the clouds magically part and rainbows shoot out of the sky . . .*

We are losing time waiting for that imaginary eighth day of the week: *Someday*. Honestly, if Someday did exist, it would be the busiest day of them all!

Now, here's a hard truth you may not want to hear: you haven't done those things on your *Someday List* because they're not a priority. That's the thing with priorities—they are what really matter to you, and if it matters to you, you'll put a specific timeline in place.

You'll remember that we talked about regret in chapter 3, and how we'll do just about anything to avoid it. Here's the most interesting thing I've found about this emotion. When psychologists dove deeper into understanding regret and how it works, what they found was the biggest regrets most people have are not centered around the mistakes they've made or their failings, but were tied to their Somedays—the goals and dreams that died because they were put on a shelf to gather dust and stink of stale air.

Let's live a life of no regrets—let's choose to stop waiting for *Someday* and set a deadline for ourselves. There's nothing like a deadline to help us prioritize the work. We think change is hard, but change is just a series of small adjustments that lead to bigger things. We cannot expect to implement life-altering changes in a week—we need to give ourselves the time to grow, but not too much time.

If you have problems being a little too flexible with your own deadlines, then get some accountability to hold you to those dates. It can be easy to push around our deadlines if there's not someone holding us accountable—it becomes easy to put our own goals and passion projects at the bottom of the people-pleasing list to be done Someday. If this is something you struggle with, you might want to consider using a formulated timeline created by someone else. For example, if you want to run a marathon, join a running group with members running the same race or use an app that helps create those deadlines for you. Find ways to create a little bit of urgency to help you get moving.

Live a *life* of

NO
REGRETS.

GOALS ARE NOT THE GOAL

Now that we understand how to set our goals, I think it's important to circle back to a concept we explored in the introduction. We don't want to live our lives fixated on goals—crossing the finish lines or earning the trophies. We need to abandon the mindset of "once I reach my goal, I'll be happy." Goals are simply landmarks on the path to our bigger lives.

Happiness isn't achieved because of a state of doing; happiness is a state of being. We can reach that state by allowing our goals to become the landmarks that guide us on our way to our much bigger purpose. Life doesn't have to be a constant strain of achieving. It can be filled with moments to savor and enjoy on the way to that big Cathedral we are dreaming of. But we can't just dream—we need to make sure that we are taking actions each and every day that feel aligned with who we are. That's what we'll be exploring next.

LIES THAT HOLD US BACK:

- I know what I want, but I can't figure out how to get it.
- I'm overwhelmed.
- Goals never seem to work for me.
- I don't even know what goals to set.

TRUTHS THAT MOVE US FORWARD:

- I have the power to design my own map to get to my big dreams.
- I am more than capable; I just need to focus on the next best step.
- I can accomplish big goals when I tie them to something meaningful.
- When I prioritize the tasks or projects with long-term benefits, I feel happier.

———————

SPRINGBOARD: Fill out your own wayfinding map. There's a blank one for you to use in the Interactive Reader's Guide.

part three

ACTION

Answers the Question: How?

six

CHOOSE TO INVEST IN YOURSELF

Standing in the living room, Marshawn intently studies the dollar bills gripped tightly in her neighbor's hands. "How much do you want?" the woman asks. "The five or the one?"

Marshawn Evans Daniels is a tall, beautifully confident friend of mine who empowers women to believe bigger in themselves and in God. But I can imagine her, standing there at the age of eleven, biting her bottom lip, deep in thought as she looks at the money clenched in the woman's fists.

Deep in conversation, I should say—conversation with herself. If we could listen in, this is what we would hear: "Which one do I deserve? I just spent hours corralling, feeding, and entertaining these two rambunctious kids. I'm exhausted, and I worked hard. I know I earned both, but I don't want to be greedy."

She knows that good girls aren't supposed to take too much, so she pushes against her instinct and reaches instead for the single dollar bill. And the woman allows it.

Marshawn now calls this moment her first life lesson: "If you allow yourself to settle for less, no one is obligated to stop you."

Wait, go back and read that again. Let that lesson wash over you and soak it in. If you are settling for less in your life, that is a choice you are making. It's not happening to you; it's happening because of you. That's some tough love, I know. But tough love is what we need, because when it comes to investing in ourselves, we women tend to struggle.

We're afraid to ask for more because we've been taught to settle for less.*

We will spend rich on our family, we will spend crazy amounts on sports and dance and God-knows-what for our kids, but we will question whether we should invest money in a self-improvement program or invest time on a passion project. *That's too much!* or *I would never spend that on myself!* I hear it all the time.

Would we deny these same things to our daughters? Or our sons? Or even our friends? When it comes to investing, we willingly, openly give to everyone but ourselves.

Here's what I want you to recognize so we can agree that you are worth the investment:

You have value far beyond what you believe.

Living an *On Purpose* life means investing in you—that's how we alter our lives to have meaning. Don't be fooled into believing it takes immense amounts of work, because it's truly not about the big actions. It's the unhurried purpose we've talked about throughout this book—it's the small steps you take each and every day. It's choosing to invest in ourselves by taking action.

THERE ARE NO SHORTCUTS

We fall in love with the idea of summiting the mountain, but we need to remember it takes effort before we can plant our flag at the top. It's tempting to believe there's a shortcut to get us to where we want to go—maybe

---

* I once had a woman ask me, "How can I be ladylike and still get what I want?" My answer back: "Redefine 'ladylike.'" Then I did a mic drop. (Not really, but that would have been incredibly satisfying.)

a gondola that will bring us straight from the flatlands and up to the top of the landmark we are looking to climb.

But there's no knowledge gained in taking the shortcut. It's crisscrossing the mountainside, making the steep climb up the rock face where we skin our knees and wear blisters into our hands, backsliding on the loose rocks—that's where we earn our knowledge and skills. We need the messy middle because without it, we gain nothing. The only way to get the satisfaction we are craving is to earn it.

We falsely believe that we want instant gratification, but truly it's when we invest in ourselves and do the work to achieve the summit that we find the truest satisfaction. Our brain is wired to prioritize seeking over finding, so whether we realize it or not, we love the thrill of the hunt—whether that's the hunt for love or success or money, that's our brain's happy place.

This is that concept of unhurried purpose we discussed way back in the introduction. We think it's in the big accomplishments and the giant leaps that happiness is hidden, but the reality is it's sitting in plain sight in our everyday lives. We simply need to look around to find it. There is immense joy *in* the journey, not just at that single moment when we complete it.

GETTING FROM HERE TO WAY OVER THERE

Let's find joy by choosing to invest in ourselves and reaching our landmarks. Back in chapter 5 we created a rough map using wayfinding, and we discovered *what* landmarks we wanted to create. But now we need to add some milestones to show us *how* to get to those landmarks. We need it to be easy and we need it to feel achievable, which means we need an Action Road Map.

Here's the truth: it's easy to get overwhelmed by the looming vision of the big landmarks off in the distance. They feel so daunting we might wonder if we can really ever reach them. Let's make this achievable. Instead of viewing those first landmarks—your Priority Landmarks—as giant goals, let's choose to see each as a series of mini goals or milestones.

Have you ever driven somewhere far away? I feel certain that the GPS or phone didn't just say, "Head to Dallas, then turn right." I'm guessing it broke the big trip down into milestones: "Go fifty-two miles, then head east" or "Take the right turn in four miles." Your big trip became easier (and you didn't get lost!) because you knew what to do each step of the way thanks to the milestones.

Just like our GPS, we can use milestones to help us reach our landmarks with ease. Milestones are designed to be much smaller (and achievable!) than landmarks. Some might be so small we may even mistake them as insignificant. But small, consistent steps are more meaningful than the occasional large leaps. These milestones are key in getting you to your landmarks.

We tend to overcomplicate things for ourselves—especially when it comes to thinking about our future—so let me show you how a really big audacious Cathedral can go from overwhelming to achievable simply by using milestones. This is just an example, but I want you to see how easy it is to start believing the future you dream about is within reach.

MAKING MAGIC HAPPEN

Let's imagine you are an eleven-year-old boy.

Oh, when I said "imagine" you thought I was joking! I wasn't. Let's make something that feels big—like achieving our goals—feel so easy that it's like playing pretend with your kids.

So you're a tween who just discovered he has magical powers, and you dream that one day you will defeat the world's most evil wizard. Let's call him . . . hmm . . . how about Voldemort? Sound good?

Okay, here's the problem: right now you are just a boy sleeping in a cupboard under your aunt's stairs, getting bullied on a regular basis by your cousin Dudley. You know that you are destined to do incredible things, but your Cathedral feels a million years away.

Let's start by wayfinding and creating some landmarks: You know that if you are to ever defeat this Voldemort guy, you'll need some support, so it seems possible that you'll need to eventually join a secret rebel society of wizards. And when you back up and think about what's practical, you decide you probably need to start using some advanced magical spells so you can defend yourself. In order to do that, you need to create a few Priority Landmarks like passing your potions class, figuring out how to pronounce *Wingardium Leviosa*, and achieving one big, heroic act.

Your wayfinding map might look like this:

| RIGHT NOW | PRONOUNCE WINGARDIUM LEVIOSA | PASS POTIONS CLASS | ACHIEVE A BIG, HEROIC ACT | LEARN ADVANCED SPELLS | JOIN SECRET SOCIETY OF REBELS | DEFEAT WORLD'S MOST EVIL WIZARD |

It's a good start, but how are you going to take action? Let's focus on one of those Priority Landmarks. Remember, these are the goals you said you could achieve in the short term. A big, heroic act will definitely increase your notoriety and help you gain some confidence, so let's brainstorm the steps you need to take to reach that landmark.

These steps can be big and small, but they should always be relevant and keep you on the right path. Generally I find that somewhere around ten steps is about right. You may have a few more or a few less, but ten is a good number to shoot for because you don't want to get bogged down in the minutiae, but you also want to clearly see what steps you need to take.

Eleven-year-old you determines the steps you need to take are:

1. Decide on wizarding supplies needed
2. Learn how Platform 9¾ works
3. Go to magical boarding school
4. Make a best friend (maybe someone with red hair?)
5. Find someone smart to help with your studies
6. Defeat a magical creature (perhaps a troll!) and build up some confidence
7. Tame a three-headed dog
8. Meet this evil Voldemort wizard
9. Keep Sorcerer's Stone safe

Before we move on, let's take a quick second to acknowledge that it's okay if you have no idea what all the steps might be—this is just a framework to help you start taking action. I find that many times, the very first step is the same: discovery work. You can always adjust your Action Road Map as you learn more about the process. After all, you never know when you might get a surprise like an invisibility cloak. For now, simply brainstorm what you think you need to do and write that down.

With your new list of steps, start grouping them together. Look for ways that the different steps can be combined together into one milestone. You might find it helpful to group steps based on the time needed to complete them. Or you might want to group together steps that are dependent on one another.

In this case we might group our steps like this:

MILESTONE 1:
RESEARCH

1. Decide on wizarding supplies needed
2. Learn how Platform 9¾ works

MILESTONE 2:
FIND SUPPORT
SYSTEM

3. Go to magical boarding school
4. Make a best friend
5. Find someone smart to help with your studies

MILESTONE 3:
BUILD UP
EXPERIENCE

6. Defeat a magical creature and build up some confidence
7. Tame a three-headed dog

MILESTONE 4:
SAVE THE
WORLD

8. Meet this evil Voldemort wizard
9. Keep Sorcerer's Stone safe

Typically four milestones are needed to get you to your landmark. Be flexible, though; you may find you need only three or you might need five. There are no rules. The only rule is that it needs to make sense to you.*

Having these milestones is incredibly important in attaining your goals and ultimately in getting you to your Cathedral. They create an opportunity to check in and assess your progress within your goal. Sometimes you have to remind yourself of how far you've come so you can show yourself how far you can go. Milestones do that for you.

Let's make sure we are continually investing in ourselves and making progress by creating measurable outcomes for each milestone, along with a deadline for reaching each one.

In our example, Milestone #1 (Research) could have the measurable outcome of having you on the train with your supplies in hand with a deadline of two weeks. Keep in mind, your milestones don't need to be evenly spaced; Milestone #2 may have a deadline of one month. Take a good look at what you need to accomplish for each and set the deadlines that feel realistic but challenging.

The biggest benefit of the Action Road Map is that it keeps us accountable. It helps ensure that we are consistently investing in our progress, and it allows us an opportunity to check in. We need to have a chance to readjust or to shift if something is not working for us. Life needs flexibility, so let's make sure and gift ourselves the grace we need. We'll be talking about this idea later in chapter 9, but it's good to start thinking about that now.

> **QUICK NOTE:** Right now, some of you might be wishing for a more real-life example of the Action Road Map. I've got you covered. I've created a realistic version for you in the back of the book in the Bonus Content section. (Please don't confuse this Bonus Content section with the dust-gathering-punch-bowl-of-an-appendix.) Head to page 199 if you want to read through that extra example right now or save it to read after you finish the book. The choice is (always) yours.

---

* Remember back in chapter 2 when we agreed we would challenge the rules? Let's bend the rules to fit you and what you think works.

WHERE ARE YOU NOW?

When we started with this example, you were a regular kid unsure of how to proceed. Now where are you? Instead of being overwhelmed by these daunting goals, you have four milestones to work toward. It's completely achievable—and you plan to reach the first one in two weeks!

That's when the real magic happens, when you start to feel like, *Okay if I take one step forward today toward this goal, after a little bit I'm going to be all the way at the end.* That is really at the heart of the whole process—making it feel like you can accomplish big things.

We need to realize that we hold the key to making the shifts we need to make. We have the ability to solve our own problems, we have the moxie to improve our lives. It's not about the Band-Aids and the quick patches. It's digging in deep and making the decision to intentionally navigate the path forward. It means we need to stop pretending there's nothing we can do.

Remember our friend Marshawn? She took that one-dollar bill from her neighbor and invested it into that lesson for herself. Fast-forward from that living room scene to two decades later—she is on the way to the airport to pick up the man she plans to marry in six short days. Her life feels incredibly sweet—then a phone call twists everything sour: her fiancé's ex-wife letting sweet Marshawn know her future husband has been cheating on her for months.

This time Marshawn didn't settle for the little amount she was offered. She called off the wedding and started investing in herself. She invested in counseling, in her health, and in her own wellness. Months later, when Mr. Ex-Fiancé came, with his tail rightly tucked between his legs, and apologized for ruining her life, she carefully chose her reaction. She replied, "You didn't ruin my life. You didn't give me my life and it's not yours to ruin."

I want to raise my hand up high and shout the word "truth" when she tells this story. Don't you? Marshawn had chosen to invest in herself and she now believed in her own value.

Marshawn told me, "You cannot get a return on an investment you never make . . . there's so many dreams we're not living. . . . We've wanted for it, but have we truly invested in it?"

If you really want the life you dream of, then you have to invest. Investment isn't always about money; it's how we choose to spend our time, where we focus our energy, and the actions we take. We have to invest in ourselves. We have to believe we have value far beyond what we have believed in the past.

"If we don't invest in ourselves, it's really a sign of self-worth," Marshawn said. We need to build up belief and self-trust in ourselves. But how do we do that? Especially if we haven't done that in the past?

Start by focusing only on that first step and then commit to action. Sounds easy enough, but I know the first step is sometimes the hardest.* Keeping up our motivation and excitement is tough, especially if we haven't done it successfully in the past. Maybe we feel we don't have the discipline to really follow through and commit. Let's let that story go.

IT'S NOT WILLPOWER YOU NEED

It's okay if you reflect back on your past and see a pattern of Shiny Object Syndrome. Maybe you have a degree you never used, or perhaps you got a wild hair and took a job that now seems crazy. No one's path is ever straight; it's always filled with curves and twists where we gather up experiences and knowledge on those detours of life.

That was certainly true for Jessica Honegger. She had done everything from getting a master's degree in education to midwifery in Bolivia to flipping homes in Texas. She had a path that seemed anything but straight. Some people might even say she needed more discipline to ever make a difference in her own life. But they would be wrong.

---

* When I first wanted to get stronger and commit to working out, I knew I just needed to schedule the first class. But I couldn't do it. I made a thousand excuses, but once I made the first step—setting up my online account—I've rarely missed a class. The first step needs to be easy because it's always the hardest to take!

Discipline and willpower are overrated. We place far too much weight on the idea of self-discipline, and we beat ourselves up for not having enough. It's easy, though, to understand why. For a long time, we've been told that our brain is split into two conflicting parts—one good part that is reasonable and knows what's best for us, and one irrational and bad.

When choosing between getting up for that 5:00 a.m. yoga class or staying in bed under the warm covers, these two fight against each other until eventually the rational side, exhausted, simply gives in. This is why we can find ourselves rolling over and pulling those warm covers back over us. We blame the decision on our lack of willpower because the bad part of us—the impulsive side of the brain—won.

Scientists called it ego depletion, and every self-proclaimed guru since has latched on to this idea that we just need to increase our willpower. It's no wonder we think of ourselves as "bad" when we go for the immediate reward over the long-term win. After all, the bad part of our brain won.* What if I told you that it's not really true? There is no bad side to your brain. The struggle in our brain isn't between good and evil but between the future and the present.

We now know that there are not two parts of our brain duking it out, but rather one single system that is designed to prioritize immediate wins over those long-term rewards. This makes sense when we think back to those studies we discovered in chapter 3. This concept of the single system in our brains is definitely connected to that research showing that we are disconnected from our future selves.

This means that if we want to take action, we need to connect more deeply with our future selves. In chapter 4 we discovered that we can see our future more clearly when we focus in on what is truly important and let go of the rest. Jessica, who chased down lots of shiny objects in her own life, experienced that clarity when she and her husband decided to adopt their son, Jack, from Rwanda.

---

* Other ways of saying this: "I'm the worst." "I'm a terrible mom/daughter/boss/friend." Can we make a pact? Can we both decide to stop calling ourselves a bad person when we don't do something 100 percent right? We've got the science to back it up, so why not give it a try?

The focus on expanding their family made the future crystal clear. Jessica was meant to be Jack's mom. She knew that without a shadow of a doubt, but she also knew she needed funds for the adoption. And money was tight. Getting her son home became her Cathedral.

Having the synergy of a bigger Cathedral to work toward helped Jessica see the actions she needed to take. She dug deep and collected those pieces of her past: living internationally, working for NGOs, seeing how entrepreneurship could be a path out of poverty. Jessica said, "Reflecting back now, I am able to see that all my seemingly circular steps were, in fact, laying a clear path for me."

She connected with two talented jewelry artisans from Uganda who were living in poverty with no marketplace for their creations. They needed sales, and Jessica needed money for her adoption. Creating a pop-up marketplace in her home seemed like the ideal solution.

That first jewelry show to raise adoption funds was just the first of many landmarks on Jessica's path. After she sold out, she got requests to do more shows so she needed to connect with more artisans. Out of this focused need, her company, Noonday Collection, was born.

She shared with me, "Really having this purpose beyond myself . . . deciding to grow our family in a nontraditional way and believing that this was the path we were meant to go on is what ultimately drove me. . . . The purpose was so much bigger." Jessica has always had a desire to create opportunities for others, especially in vulnerable communities. Her past was always leading her there; she just needed to start taking steps to get to that big dream.

Jessica has continued to invest in herself by taking action and it shows. Her business has grown continuously. Today she partners with over 4,500 artisans and has been able to touch the lives of about 20,000 people in the countries where she works.

Remember the blast radius we talked about in chapter 2? We may start small, but our ability to affect the world around us is infinite. We can easily see that in Jessica's story. But here's the catch: it's not big lightning-bolt moments that define us—it's the ability to choose to act. Tiny steps that feel small at first but build over time and create new breadcrumbs.

Jessica firmly believes, "We anticipate our future by how we remember our past. So when we can create these new stories of success and confidence . . . [we] can actually anticipate a new future for [our]selves."

ANTICIPATING YOUR FUTURE

We can anticipate new futures for ourselves. I want you to take that in. We have the ability to choose: we don't need to wait for motivation—we can create it for ourselves. We don't need willpower or discipline. We just need to create new stories of success for ourselves. If we develop cycles of self-belief and self-trust, our brain will want to take action.

When I hear about that new brain research about how our brain prioritizes immediate wins over long-term wins, I realize it explains why some people are able to win the battle for motivation. They clearly see and connect their actions with their future.

But—and this is key here—if your future feels disconnected, as it does for so many people, you've got a playbook for how you can make the connection. It's not willpower that's needed—it's a strategy for action. To get motivated and to invest in ourselves, we need to connect our choices with ourselves in the future.

When we struggle and fail to follow through on promises we make to ourselves, the excuses usually focus on an issue within us. According to the Mayo Clinic, some of the most common excuses people make are "I'm too lazy," "I think it's going to be boring," or "I'm self-conscious." These aren't excuses about the tasks; these are judgments we are making about ourselves being bad. We don't trust ourselves to actually follow through and do the work.

Building self-trust is an arduous process with many, many steps— here's both of them:

1. Start implementing a small healthy habit for yourself— something that's an easy win.
2. Repeat.

We want to establish new breadcrumbs—a pattern of following through and trusting ourselves. We know that once we see a pattern, we love to keep it going. If we create a consistent rhythm of believing in ourselves, that will become a new pattern we easily accept.

These are small, tiny wins, so small they might not feel like much. They may even feel insignificant. But the more you keep them up, the more credibility and trust you build in yourself.

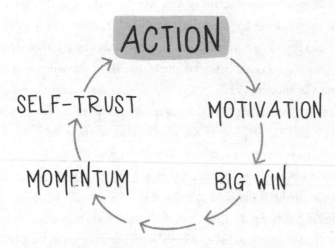

In time, these habits help to establish a new identity for yourself. You are no longer a slob; you are a person who makes your bed each morning. You are no longer the worst at money; you are a person who spends ten minutes reconciling your accounts twice a week. You aren't incompetent; you are a person who reads three pages of a book before bedtime every night.

Change your identity, and everything else changes as well.

THE FIRST THREE MILES

Unathletic. That's how Dorothy Beal would have described herself growing up. She didn't even have the stamina for a full lap at the track. In college, a never-ending cycle of poor eating, sleeping, and drinking away her worries led to what felt like rock bottom. After some encouragement from her mom, she decided running would be a better way to deal with her stress.

"I definitely was one of the last people that my friends would have ever thought would become a runner, much less a marathoner," Dorothy admitted to me. The word *marathoner* here might not do an adequate job of truly explaining who she is and how she creates an impact.

Dorothy has run almost fifty marathons (and counting) while also writing and representing some of the world's largest health publications and brands promoting her foundational belief: runners come in all shapes and sizes, and if you run, you have a runner's body. That's a strong purpose from a woman who once believed she didn't have the willpower to run a lap around the soccer pitch.

For a long time in her life, she never ran past the first few miles—they felt difficult and exhausting as she trudged down the road. "But I started to notice that after runs, I felt better mentally and physically," she shared. "It just kind of snowballed, and I focused on that *after feeling*, which is what got me through my first marathon."

In looking at her patterns, Dorothy realized there was a sweet spot on her runs. Those first three miles were always her toughest—and even today they're still the worst—but once she gets those behind her, the runs feel freeing. The problem was she had spent the majority of her life in those first three miserable miles.

It wasn't until she created a cycle of self-trust that she could even see that feeling that came with running. Now "I focus on that *after feeling* versus the feeling of those first three worst miles. . . . I also just give myself permission to go out there, and only run one mile. . . . [But] I honestly don't think I've ever done that . . . more often than not, I have more to give than I thought." She's created a mental habit circle, proving to herself again and again that she is able to achieve much more than she thought possible. And that self-trust grows.

Small wins build up and help you gain momentum for big victories. "I think it spills over into your everyday life," explained Dorothy. "When you can push through those low points for something as simple as running, then it makes it easier to push through other things. And when you believe in yourself in that area, you can believe in yourself for other things."

When you create a cycle of self-trust, it gives you the momentum to keep moving forward. We're all going to have days that we fall off the horse, where we just can't get up and do our meditation, or we justify pulling the covers back on because it's too cold for our morning walk. We all have bad days or days when we question if we've got what it takes. But if you continually show up—show up for yourself—you will establish that pattern of belief in yourself. That, yes, maybe today was hard, but you can pick it back up tomorrow. You are not defined by one bad day.

BEING THE UNDERDOG

One of the other big stumbling blocks I see when it comes to taking action is the idea that we don't know what we are doing. We don't want to look like we are starting at the bottom, so we choose not to start at all.

We love the story of the underdog . . . unless we *are* the underdog. No one likes being smack dab in the messy middle; no one enjoys being the one who doesn't know what they are doing. But that's part of everyone's journey.

Stephen King didn't wake up knowing how to write a bestselling book—he was living in a trailer working as a janitor at the age of twenty-four. Vera Wang didn't instinctively know how to sew her designs—she starting figuring it out at the age of forty. Julia Child didn't know how to cook an egg until she started taking lessons in her thirties.

Here's the biggest secret in life: No one has it all together. No one—not a single one of us, no matter what our impressive bio says or how amazing our life looks on paper—has it all figured out. We are all lifelong students, fumbling our way through, doing our very best.

So why is it so hard to admit that?

PUT ON YOUR LEARNER PLATES

The horn blared as a red car screamed past me and cut me off, nearly clipping my front fender. I felt my breath catch in my throat as the driver shoved his meaty arm out the window and angrily flicked up his middle finger with the precision of a drill sergeant. I slowly felt the air escape my lungs and noticed that my hands clenching the steering wheel were white-knuckled, gripped so tightly that I had to pry them open. "Congrats," my instructor smirked. "You just got your first bird. Next time you need to look left before you turn, okay?"

I was so close to my sixteenth birthday that I could almost taste the cake. I was just starting to learn how to navigate the Texas roads. I was nervous, and my driving showed it, but within a few weeks I had my license and got to dip my toes into some real freedom.

Somehow, though, one year later at the age of seventeen, I found myself once again learning how to drive. This time the steering wheel I clenched was on the opposite side of the car and I was trying to figure out how in the world to use a stick shift with my left hand. My family had moved to Scotland, and I needed to be able to drive on the other side of the road in my new country. I think my dad got a manual shift just to challenge me—that's kinda his style.

I remember sitting at a three-lane roundabout, terrified as the cars whizzed round and round. I eased up on the clutch, punched down on the gas, and stuttered the car into the busy intersection where, thanks to me flooding the engine with gas, it promptly died. A bright red car deftly swerved to miss me, and as it passed the driver threw his arm out the window—and waved. "You'll do better next time," he called out cheerily.

Two very different experiences learning to drive a car. Both times I was nervous and uncertain, but one time I received a lot more grace. Do you wonder why? In Scotland, you are required to have an L-plate on your car—a white square with a red L on the front and back of the vehicle to show everyone else on the road that you are a learner . . . a newbie . . . someone just figuring things out.

I admit, I was embarrassed—no, mortified—to put that plate on the car and argued that I didn't need it. But having that *L* allowed everyone else on the road to know that I needed more room for mistakes, more space to try new things, and the freedom to fail.

We could all benefit from having learner plates pinned onto our chests because we are all fumbling our way through life—every single one of us. The funny thing is that admitting you are simply a student, doing your best to figure things out, is actually an advantage. We just have to choose to see our lack of knowledge and experience as a benefit instead of a burden.

I love how Neil Gaiman, who's won almost every award possible for writing, spoke about inexperience in his commencement speech to the University of the Arts. He gave this solidly good advice:

> When you start out . . . you have no idea what you are doing.
>
> This is great. People who know what they are doing know the rules, and know what is possible and impossible.
>
> You do not. And you should not. The rules on what is possible and impossible . . . were made by people who had not tested the bounds of the possible by going beyond them. And you can.
>
> If you don't know it's impossible, it's easier to do. And because nobody's done it before, they haven't made up rules to stop anyone doing that again, yet.

Do you see what I see in that speech? I see freedom from those rules we are always trying to live by. Glorious freedom that's there once you accept that you don't know what you are doing and stop listening to anyone who says there are rules and limits. Not knowing what is impossible makes everything possible—that is the gift of being naive.

Beautiful boundless naiveté.

Greta Gerwig latched on to this idea of "embracing the not knowing" with *Lady Bird*, a film that garnered rave reviews and Oscar nominations for her as a first-time solo writer and director. That's not to say she didn't have nerves going into the project. She confided to director and friend Rebecca Miller that she was worried that, because she had never directed before, she didn't have the "sixth sense about what [she would] need" from her actors and crew.

Miller shared this advice:

> I'm gonna tell you what Mike Nichols told me: "Don't let this pass you by. You will only have the chance to not know what you're doing once."
>
> And there's a real power in that because you don't even know what there is to be scared of yet. And you will learn and you will become paralyzed by certain things later, but right now keep your innocence intact because it will allow you to make choices that later you'll never have the naiveté to be so brave to make.

When you don't know the rules, you aren't confined by them. You can step over the line and test your boundaries in ways that allow you to bend them a bit. It's okay to wing it—in fact, allow your wings to stretch and extend to their full size. Flap them a bit and see where they'll take you. But you can't do that unless you get out of your own way and decide to do it.

BEING A BEAUTIFUL MESS

Asking questions, feeling unsure and vulnerable, doesn't make you weak. I understand, though, that it makes you feel a little naked and exposed. In the end, we are all human and we're not designed to be perfect, and it's okay to go out and look a little foolish. Only fools win in the end, because they are the only ones willing to risk the boundaries of what they do and don't know, so be proud of being foolish. It means you are putting yourself out there. The true fools are the ones who never try at all.

Funny enough, being vulnerable and embracing your learner status is something others will respect about you. We worry about looking silly, but research suggests that there's a discrepancy in how we view our own

When it comes to *investing,*

DOUBLE DOWN ON YOU.

vulnerability compared to how others perceive it. Studies indicate that we tend to think it makes us appear inadequate and weak—a mess, so to speak. But when others see our vulnerability, even if it's the same trait we're criticizing in ourselves, they tend to perceive something quite different and even alluring. This phenomenon is called "the beautiful mess effect."

We will criticize ourselves for the same thing that we sympathize with in someone else. Somehow we are able to find compassion for someone else's vulnerabilities over our own. This helps explain the comparison trap we talked about falling into earlier in this book, and it helps us understand why we feel the need for the mask of perfectionism.

Why is it that we can be so forgiving to someone else for their vulnerabilities and yet so self-loathing when it comes to those same vulnerabilities in ourselves? We need to learn to give ourselves permission to venture out and try something new.

What would happen if we chose to get out of our own way? What if we decided to stop waiting until we have all the answers (we'll never have all the answers!), and we stopped waiting for the motivation, and we just chose to take action?

There are fears and there are lies that latch on to you and tell you it cannot be done. But it can. It just takes action. We'll be tackling those in our next chapter, but here's what I want you to remember before we move on: *when it comes to investing, double down on you.*

LIES THAT HOLD US BACK:

- I have no willpower.
- Where do I even begin?
- I don't know what I'm doing.
- I could never spend that on myself.

TRUTHS THAT MOVE US FORWARD:

- When I remind myself how far I've come, I can see how far I can go.
- My big dreams are achievable when I break them down.
- Accepting that I'm a first-timer means I can create my own rules.
- An investment in myself shows that I believe in my own value.

SPRINGBOARD: Build motivation by creating a cycle of self-trust. Decide on a simple habit you can repeat every day for two weeks.

seven

CHOOSE TO RELEASE YOUR FEARS

There wasn't a cloud in sight; it had been a gorgeous sunny day. I had just met up with John for a quick lunch date before running to pick up the two kids from preschool and then rushing over to get their hair cut. I felt light and happy like a helium balloon—bouncy and full. Laughing, I grabbed ahold of Kate's arms and swung her up to my chest.

And then I saw him.

And, just like that, my balloon popped and shredded into a thousand tiny little pieces of latex shrapnel.

Hunched over, standing outside the door of the salon with both hands shoved in his pockets, stood my husband. He was looking somewhat dazed—like he'd just stepped out of a dark room and into the bright sunlight. He didn't say a word but simply looked me in the eyes. And somehow, I knew. In the secret language of marriage, sometimes you don't have to say a word to know that your world is suddenly crashing down.

I had just seen him two hours earlier where we had felt so light and easy, picking food off each others' plates, teasing each other. And now we stood three feet apart, uncertain of what words we could possibly say.

A tumble of words fell out of my mouth, and I flinched at the sound of their unintended sharpness, "What are you doing here?"

But I already knew. There was no other reason why my husband would be loitering outside of a strip mall on a Thursday afternoon. We were in the middle of the Great Recession and there were a solid handful of our friends who were standing in the long line of the unemployed. I understood that he had just joined the back of that line.

But it didn't make sense—not in my mind—and I couldn't seem to reconcile it. I shook my head and opened my mouth like a fish out of water, hoping to say something to make it all right.

I pulled him into me and wrapped my arms around him while Kate clung to me like a baby monkey in between us and Jack gripped on to my leg. "We will be okay," I whispered hoarsely. "We will be okay."

But I didn't really believe it. How would we possibly be okay in the middle of a recession with our one breadwinner out of a job? I could almost feel the icy cold fingers of fear circling around us—and I could definitely see it in my husband's eyes.

Fear.

We think it's the thing that holds us back. But what if it's exactly what we need to push ourselves forward? I've told the story a thousand times of how I decided to start my own business—that I was pulled to create a life for my family because of a single conversation my husband and I had while we were thousands of miles apart.

But that's not the full story. Every story needs a villain—a foil for our hero. For me, that was fear. Fear was the great motivator to give me that extra push and drive to really believe I had it in me to build a business and create a lifestyle for my family.

BREAK DOWN THE WALL

I once heard this metaphor where fear was described as a wall and on one side—the side we are on—is where we are comfortable. It's where we feel like we know what we are doing and life feels easy. Maybe we should say "easier" here instead because it may not be the life we truly want, but it *is* comfortable.

On the other side of that wall, though, is freedom—freedom to be vulnerable, freedom to put ourselves out there, freedom to explore the possibilities, freedom to be true to who we really want to be.

For many people, they see that towering wall of fear and believe they are simply stuck. There's no way to climb over it or get around it. They give in and choose to become comfortable in their own discomfort. Even though they desperately long for the freedom on the other side, they think they cannot get there because that damn wall is blocking their way.

Grab your sledgehammer, sister.

Avoiding the fear and pretending it's not there isn't working. We cannot bury our heads in the sand and continue acting like it's okay to be unsatisfied. We need to do a little inner work to look at this fear of ours and examine why it's there, and then we need to learn to trust ourselves so we can bust that wall down (or at least knock a you-sized hole in it).

WHAT ARE YOU SCARED OF?

There are two kinds of fear: survival fears and perception fears. Survival fears are fears of things like death, getting hurt, or not being able to take care of your basic needs.* Survival fear is a much-needed part of our brain. After all, it's what helps us stay alive; it's what allowed us to avoid the saber-tooth tigers while living in our caves all those years ago.

Perception fears, though, are different. Perception fears aren't really life threatening, but they manifest in exactly the same way as survival fears: our palms get sweaty, we feel short of breath, and our mouth is suddenly as dry as the Sahara Desert.

When we push outside of our comfort zone, our brain senses unfamiliarity, so it throws out a loud, jarring alarm, ultimately giving you that sensation

---

* Basic needs are food, shelter, air . . . losing your cell phone doesn't count here.

of fear. We assume that it's our intuition sending us a sign that we should just avoid the risk. So we decide, instead, to hunker down in our comfort zone.

Honestly, our threat system is great at keeping us alive and avoiding stepping into a busy intersection, but it's not so great at distinguishing between real physical threats and perceived risks—especially social fears like fear of failure, disappointing others, or embarrassment.

Let me put this idea of fear and risk into perspective for you. The number-one fear that most people have is public speaking.* An activity, we can both agree, that is really not that risky—while people might judge your stage presence or ability to keep your audience awake, I feel relatively certain neither of those will actually kill you.

Just to be certain, I pulled up a list from the National Safety Council and found that there are a lot of risky behaviors most of us don't think twice about—like driving a car. You don't stress about hopping in your car and going around the corner to the store, do you? You don't obsess about what could happen on the way, but interestingly, the odds of dying in a car accident over the course of your lifetime is 1 in 107. The odds of dying of stage fright? Zero. Trust me, I checked the list twice just to be sure.**

Perception fears are not life-threatening (even though they may feel that way in the moment), but we think they are because they are steeped in self-doubt.

THREE SEEDS OF SELF-DOUBT

We all have times where we question ourselves—even people who appear absolutely confident. Self-doubt comes from a story that we tell ourselves *about ourselves*—a story that is filled with false truths, which take root and become our negative bedrock beliefs.

---

* Also discovered in this same study? Democrats are nearly twice as likely as Republicans to have a fear of clowns. I don't know what that has to do with anything we're talking about here, but it was just too odd of a statistic not to share with you. You're welcome.
** I did, however, also learn that your odds of being legally executed are 1 in 119,012. I hope this helps you sleep better at night knowing that probably won't happen either.

Cognitive behavior therapists categorize these core beliefs into three categories: unlovability, helplessness, and worthlessness. In other words, your perception fears bloom from three little seeds of self-doubt:

I am unlovable.
I am helpless.
I am worthless.

Surprised? I was when I really dug into the research, but then I started to see a pattern. (I may have mentioned to you our brains love patterns.) If you start to go through the lists of all the different social perception fears, you'll start to see they easily fit into one of these three categories.

I am unlovable.	I am helpless.	I am worthless.
Fear of disappointing others	Fear of looking foolish	Fear of being inadequate
Fear of being judged	Fear of commitment	Fear of failure
Fear of getting hurt	Fear of the unknown	Fear of losing control
Fear of loneliness	Fear of missing out	Fear of rejection
Fear of being broken	Fear of change	Fear of being vulnerable

Isn't it amazing that there are only three stories at the heart of our fears? We conjure an entire world around our own false truths, so they seem much bigger. But at their core, our fears are all rooted around these three little seeds.

We could spend an entire book talking about each and every one of the fears we may have. That list above is just a sampling of a few—and you could even argue that some of the fears bridge more than one, so let's go straight to the root of this fear problem—the stories.

I AM UNLOVABLE

We all are looking to be seen and heard, so it's no surprise that worrying about being unlovable is a seed of self-doubt.

We worry so much about what everyone else thinks. Here's a hard truth I want you to hold tightly to: if you live your life trying to avoid disappointing others, you will end up only disappointing yourself.

People are going to judge—there's no getting around that. They'll judge based on their own limited life experiences that have absolutely nothing to do with you. That puts you at the mercy of their unreliable and completely biased perspectives. You will never find your value in another person's opinion. You have to find it in yourself.

Without question, *I am unlovable* is my own main seed of doubt. Even with my uncanny ability to kill all plants (sometimes even artificial ones), I could bloom an entire botanical garden filled with this story.

As a middle child, I hungrily ate up the crumbs of any words of affirmation that fell my way, and I basked in the role of being the family peacekeeper. For years I wore my people-pleaser badge with pride, shining it up any chance I could get.

I'd like to tell you that I don't plant this seed anymore, that there was a spectacular moment in my life where it all changed. I know that would please you—and I am a people pleaser after all. But it's not true. Our little seeds of self-doubt don't fully go away—most of us had them planted long ago into our subconscious, so they have long taproots like weeds.

But what I've discovered is, if you understand the way you think and the stories you tell yourself, you can own your mindset. I started to see this seed not as an obstacle but as an opportunity. I've learned to take my fear of disappointing others and being judged and turn it into a superpower. Let me share what this looks like for me:

Many times when I go to large charitable business events, the room is filled with people from corporations, banks, and real estate agencies. Most of the people in the room are wearing suits and ties, a lot of them sporting gray hair. I show up as me: no suit, no tie. But I'll slide up into a group and join the conversation.

"Who are you here with?" they ask me, assuming I'm an employee of one of the marquee names.

I smile and tell them, "I own my own business."

What happens next has been repeated more times than I can count.

"Oh, how nice," they reply, looking as if they want to pat me on the head like a child. "What does your husband do?"

At that moment, I pull myself up to my full five-foot-three height, look them squarely in the eye, and say:

"He works for me."

Then I give them a full two-second lull because I know what to expect—the furrowed brow along with the look of utter confusion—they don't know what to say. So I fill the pause by kindly explaining how I run a successful conscious company that donates and operates with philanthropy at its heart—that's why I'm in the room. And yes, I'm the CEO, while my husband loves working as my CMO. I am not a hobbyist; I'm a proud businesswoman.

The reactions of these people in the room don't make me mad or frustrate me. I just know that I have stepped outside of the circle of their idea of "normal." No one would question if a woman worked for her husband, but my lifestyle doesn't fit their expected pattern.

There was a time, when being asked how my husband supports my "little" business, I would have taken it as a judgment—a clear reminder that I'm an unlovable person because I don't fit in. But I have untangled that story for myself; I've pulled it up, roots and all.

I've learned that if I live in a way that triggers others, it has nothing to do with me and everything to do with them. I am happy that it gives me a chance to educate and explain that I'm not really an outlier to society; I'm part of the evolution.

Rejection, or someone not understanding your special brand of magic, doesn't mean a thing and isn't a reflection of you.

We have to stop blaming everyone else and worrying about what they will think. You are stealing from your own happiness—other people are not your roadblock and do not determine your value. You don't need everyone to buy in on your dream. But *you* have to choose to go all in on *you*.

I AM HELPLESS

When we think we don't have choices, we lose faith in our own abilities and we begin to define ourselves as *stuck*: stuck in a dead-end job, a toxic relationship, a no-win situation, or whatever it is that makes us believe we have no choice.

Feeling stuck is nothing more than a temporary obstacle life throws at you to challenge you and to make you feel less powerful and in control than you really are. The truth is that you are in control. We always have the ability to choose; we just sometimes forget that we do. We may not love the choices, they may not be easy decisions, but the options are always there—even when we can't see them right away.

We think the opposite of "stuck" is "unstuck." We need to realize the opposite of stuck is action. Small steps, tiny steps, any steps will move you away from being stuck. We tend to undervalue the power of a single step, but that's really all we need to get us started on our path to our landmark.

Maggie Beaudouin is an incredibly talented publicist, landing her clients in some of the world's most prestigious magazines and TV shows. She works with a mixture of tenacity and grace, gaining the respect of everyone she works with . . . everyone but her boss at her PR agency. Time and time again, she brought the company recognition and accolades, but she consistently found herself undervalued and overworked. Worst of all? She felt stuck.

The option of starting something new didn't seem like a choice. After all, she has rent to pay and people who count on her. Caught in a loop of not wanting to disappoint her clients but tired of being disappointed herself, she didn't see any way out.

Maggie and I met and talked about her options: she could get comfortable in the discomfort of her current life, or she could see that she was not completely helpless in choosing the life she wanted.

In a moment like this, when we have these big obstacles in our path, they can appear so large we believe we cannot possibly see around them.

That sensation of being stuck brings in the fear and feelings of helplessness. We can choose, though, to step back and take a good look from a different point of view. We can change our perspective.

Maggie and I talked about the rent and the responsibilities; we looked at each of the obstacles from top to bottom, sideways and upside down. That's when we began to see the tiny little cracks and fissures, which is how we knew we could get her unstuck.

She did all the work; I simply helped her see possibilities. She told me, "I threw those windows wide open, and I'm happier than I've ever been." Leaving her old company and finding a flexible job that will allow her to pursue an advanced degree is the best decision she could have made. "I work so well with [my new boss]. The pay is less, but I would trade it any day for the happiness I have now."

When we make choices based on faith in ourselves rather than fear, we take ownership of our own happiness.

No matter what changes you need to make in life to gain success, nothing happens until you decide. Those changes won't make themselves, and you can't pull yourself up out of that rut until you make the choice. Absolutely nothing happens until you decide. You are not helpless; you just need to discover your options.

I AM WORTHLESS

Remember back in chapter 4 when we talked about the two kinds of perfectionists? We have the Idealists, who never seem to start, and we have the Strivers, the ones who start but set impossibly high standards. Both perfectionists cling tightly to the "I am worthless" story and combat it by trying to make everything absolutely perfect.

They are constantly exhausting themselves, battling against failure—or looking like a failure—at every turn. They sweat away keeping it all together so that everyone else looks at them and thinks they've got it figured out. Meanwhile, they lie awake at night scared their secret will be revealed: that they're really just human like the rest of us, completely fallible and doing their best to not drop the ball.

We often confuse comfort with safety. It's easy to get caught up in the question of, Will I fail?

My husband, John, is without question a Striver constantly battling against his "I am unworthy" story. It wasn't surprising he hesitated as we talked about moving to a bigger life. When I stood in our kitchen and declared that I would be an entrepreneur, he didn't feel quite as confident as I did.*

The safe bet, he thought, was for him to move to another corporate job with almost no travel. He hated his new position—it was soul sucking. So when he found himself laid off and standing outside that hair salon, he told me, "It's one thing to fail when you are going after your dream, but when you compromise and fail? It's crushing."

We can allow our fears to run wild in our minds, wreaking havoc and making such a loud ruckus we can barely remember why we wanted to step away from comfort in the first place. Sometimes we just have to take the leap because we believe in ourselves more than we believe the noise.

We have to believe that we are worthy: worthy of the good, worthy of the respect, worthy of making the attempt. Because even when we fail, we learn. When we fail because we never try, we gain nothing at all.

No one really wants to fail. No one goes out there with an idea or a dream and thinks, "You know what? It would be really great if I failed. Man, I'd learn a lot from that." But here's the truth: there's not a success story out there that doesn't include life-changing adversity. I'm going to let you in on a little secret: if you aren't failing from time to time, you are failing.

Listen, the universe is messy. If you try to hold on to a specific way of doing things or how things will unfold, you might feel as if you've failed. But you haven't. Find the opportunities hidden in the pile of manure.

---

* Remember, I had zero business experience, so I'm not surprised he worried about it failing.

Here's the pony I've learned from that season: failure, not progress, is the truest sign of growth. If you are failing, it means you are pushing yourself instead of staying in that comfortable place on the other side of the wall.

Experiencing failure doesn't mean *you* are a failure. It means you stuck your neck out there, you took a chance, and it didn't work out. That doesn't make you a failure; it makes you human. Failures become the breadcrumbs—the proof that we are resilient and can overcome obstacles. If we are resilient, we can become brave.

BRAVE VS. FEARLESS

Doubt is still present even when you are on the right track. Fear is not a sign that you are on the wrong track—in fact, it can be a sign that you are exactly where you need to be to uplevel.

Why, then, do we believe we need to be fearless?

Being fearless means the absence of fear—you have no fear; you are fear-*less*. And in some cases, yes, you are fearless. In places in your life that feel easy, you live confidently—fearlessly, if you will. We don't worry every single time we step in the shower that we'll slip and fall; we don't stress about whether the sky is falling when it rains.

We live fearlessly throughout our day, but that's not possible all the time. Fear, in fact, is a very powerful, very necessary emotion. Fear lives within us to keep us safe—it's in our DNA to naturally feel fear. If we didn't, we would lean too far forward when looking over the Grand Canyon, or we wouldn't think twice about jumping off the roof instead of using a ladder when hanging the Christmas lights. We need fear. So we need to stop thinking of fear as the enemy and focus, instead, on how we can make fear push us. That's what being brave is all about.

Being brave doesn't mean you don't have fear—a brave soldier runs into battle not because she has an absence of fear, but because she's got the mental and moral strength to overcome that fear in order to protect others. Being brave means you are so much stronger than if you were merely fearless because it means you've overcome those things that scare you.

Think back on a time you did a small act of bravery. For me, it's eight-year-old Tanya standing, in a bright-blue bathing suit with rainbow stripes, frozen at the edge of the high dive. I can still remember peering down at the water far below and being so scared that I could hardly catch my breath. Slowly, I shifted my feet so that I stood tiptoe and bounced once, twice, and made the plunge.

It wasn't a beautiful dive, but the moment my body hit the cool water that adrenaline rush hit me—the thrill of overcoming that fear. And the desire to make my way back up that long ladder to do it all again, this time with grace. That, my friend, is being brave. Without question, you've had small moments of intense bravery in your own life too. Don't you want to feel that again? Let's do this—let's start living bravely and overcoming fear to make your big goals a reality.

LIVING BRAVELY

The objective isn't complete and unwavering confidence, but the skilled management of your limiting beliefs and self-doubts. We need to learn to trust ourselves that we'll be okay even if we get rejected or if we fail. And then . . . we need to act in the presence of fear.

This is really a practice of mindfulness: we don't pretend the fear isn't there; we want to notice the fear and be aware of our reaction to it. It's taking intentional risks. Notice that word *intention* here. It's not about risk-taking; it's choosing to take meaningful risks.

Let's truly learn to assess the risk—remember, we are trying to get from point A to point Z. We want to believe it's a beautiful, straight-and-easy line, but our map looks more like this:

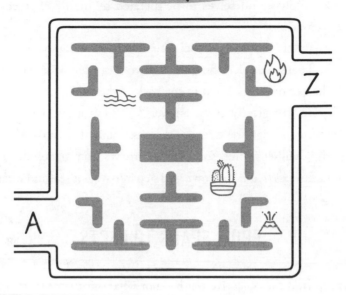

It's not about leaping off the cliff; it's about standing on the edge, taking time to assess whether you really can make the jump—and then giving yourself a running start. Let's look around and see: *Is there actually a bridge a little down the road, or is there a place where the jump is just a bit narrower?* Or maybe it's not even a jump at all. Maybe it's finding a path that winds down into the canyon and makes its way up the other side.

It's okay that there's some fear there, but let's choose to assess the risk. Let's look at it from a different angle or perspective and then decide what the best approach might be. Make a plan so you feel more confident about jumping in.

Here's the incredibly obvious truth about risk: risk is scary. We don't want to fail, we don't want to fall on our face or look foolish, so we allow the risk to outweigh the rewards. Instead of pushing past our fears, we let all those negative *what-ifs* stop us dead in our tracks. Those are our false truths that are steeped in our own biases and negative core beliefs.

Scientists are constantly challenging beliefs with the goal of finding the *objective truth*—a truth that is not defined by emotions or feelings but by evidence. What if we chose to find the objective truth about our fears rather than allowing ourselves to be dictated by highly charged, highly unreliable emotions?

"Do whatever it takes to not fool yourself into thinking something is true, that is not. That's the scientific method," said astrophysicist Neil deGrasse Tyson. "The answer is not listed in the back of the book. . . . There's not [a] teacher's guide that gives you the answers." You test it out, you experiment knowing there's no right or wrong—there is simply the truth. We all know that the truth will set us free, so let's free ourselves from the bindings of fear. Let's cut those ropes that tie us down and step into what is real and what is true.

FROM FEARS TO FACTS

We want to find the objective truth—not what our threat system tells us, but what is actually real. Let's use the scientific method to discover it. I've created a blueprint based on the scientific method that we can use when we are struggling to move past fear. I've shared it on page 143, but let me guide you through it now.

Observation: What is it you are feeling afraid of doing?

There's no judgment here. Remember, we all feel fear, so there's no shame in accepting that you are scared. Write it out and see how it feels to see those words on paper.

Hypothesis: Is this a perception fear or a survival fear?

Here's a Nancy Drew tip for you to help you solve this question: perception fears like to disguise themselves so they seem bigger than they really are—the same way the mean girl in seventh grade liked to puff out her chest when trying to make you feel insignificant. *Exactly the same way.*

They dress up and pretend to be life threatening, even when they aren't. Here's a quick example of how that looked for us as John left corporate America and I started my own business:

SURVIVAL FEAR: *We won't be able to pay the mortgage and will find ourselves homeless on the streets!*

But really it was the fear of potential embarrassment if this new venture failed:

PERCEPTION FEAR: *What will everyone think if we have to move out of our house?*

Take a good look at your fear and make a guess or two (or three!) as to what types of fear you are experiencing. Is it fear of rejection or commitment or failure? There may be more than one.

Experiment: What are the worst-case scenarios?

Yes, scenarios, as in more than one. Your mind likes to run wild through the hallways, so just let it. Write down all the terrible, horrible things that might happen. Make the list and then ask yourself, Is that really everything? And then write down a few more—you know they are there.

List out every single *what-if* thought you've had, every concern your well-meaning friends have mentioned, and every nightmare scene you've played through late at night while lying in bed. Trust me, you'll feel better confronting them in the light of day rather than letting them lurk in the dark pockets of your brain.

Analyze: Is this really the worst that can happen?

When you go through that long list of worst-case scenarios, ask yourself: Is this really the worst thing that can happen? Are there ways that you could minimize the impact? Is it something that you could recover from? With our earlier example, that fear of not being able to pay the mortgage—would you really be homeless? Or would you be able to find a place to stay temporarily? Sure, your childhood bedroom that your mom converted into an art studio ten minutes after you left for college isn't ideal, but it could work as a place to stay if need be. Wouldn't it?

Elizabeth Grojean, founder of the healthy, sustainable, conscious-living brand Baloo Living, told me, "The decision to launch [my company] was really a series of small decisions, and each one was a chance to back out and give in to self-doubt." She knew the opportunity to start her company would build on her gifts, so she embraced stepping through that wall of fear to the other side. It wasn't easy, but like her brand, she did it consciously.

Taking time to step back and fully look at her fear made her realize, "At each moment of indecision, I reminded myself of the worst-case scenario: the company would fail to take off, I'd realize I wasn't cut out for entrepreneurship, and I would have to move back to New York City and get a job. I could appreciate then, and now, that my worst-case scenario would have still been a very fortunate outcome, and there was nothing really to fear, except success!"

When Elizabeth took time to analyze her fear, she discovered that she could choose to see that there was an opportunity.

Observation: What can you control versus not control?

Remember, we can only really control our own behaviors and reactions. We have no control over what other people say, how they will react, what they do, or what they post on the internet. These are things we are powerless to change. We can either sit around worrying about what other people might say (many of them possibly knowing nothing about us) or we can take action. And by action, I mean focus on what we can control.

In the list you created of the fears and then the actions you can take, how much of this fear is within your control? I'm going to give you a hint: all of it. Yes, on that list of fears there may be some things that you cannot control, such as what others say or do, but you can control how *you* react to them. When you analyzed each of those fears, did you see a pattern of power? You can make choices. You can choose to minimize those fears or even to recover from them. We believe fear has the power to make us feel stuck, but we are always in control of how we react. Look back at the list of fears and scratch through the ones that don't have the power to control you.

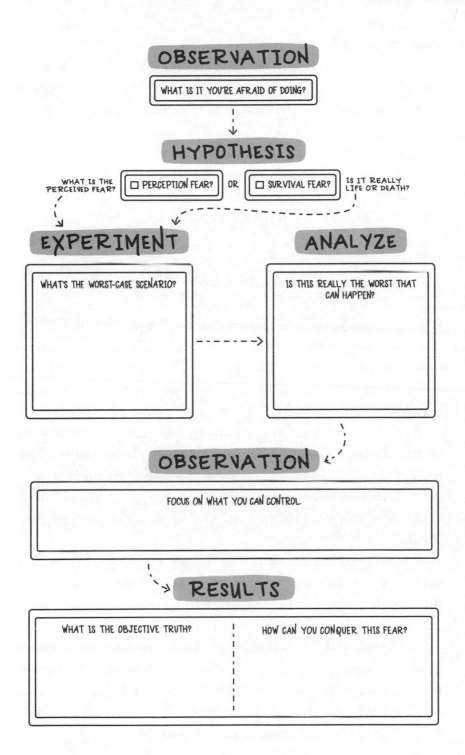

Results: What is the objective truth?

You have to accept that the world isn't conspiring for you to fail. I promise you, it's not. Right now you have a 100 percent survival rate of all the things you did in your past, even when you were scared. Don't let your challenges or insecurities get the best of you.

What is real and true about your fear? There's an objective truth you have uncovered through this process, so write it down. Now that you've gone through the evidence and tested your hypothesis, what is it you are really afraid of and how can you conquer it?

LET'S GET EXCITED

Fear will always be there. We cannot escape it, but we can reframe it. We don't have to always fixate on the dangers. Fear can be our body's reaction to something bigger that's coming around the corner in our lives. It doesn't necessarily mean we have to run and hide. Fear can mean we are on the right path.

In fact, when it comes to stress, anxiety, and excitement, the physical experiences your body goes through are very similar: faster heartbeat, high levels of stress hormones, boosts in your adrenaline, and an increase in sweat. Essentially, your body reacts the same to fear as it does to sitting at the top of that roller coaster when you are eagerly, excitedly awaiting that drop.

Instead of choosing to see that feeling as a sign of excitement, we try our best to tamp it down. When we start to feel the sweat forming on our palms or when we notice the army of butterflies in our stomachs, our go-to reaction is to tell ourselves to simply relax.

A Harvard Business School study found that about 90 percent of people think that when they are confronted with anxiety or fear, they should simply tell themselves to calm down. I don't know about you, but any time that I get worked up and someone tells me to relax, it completely backfires. It just fires me up more. Just me? I didn't think so.

Fear is *not* your enemy.

FEAR

can be your *biggest*

ALLY.

Alison Woods Brooks, who led the study, made the connection that it's an easier shift for the brain to move from anxiety to excitement since both are highly charged emotions. It's more difficult to swing from a charged-up emotion to calm. In other words, when you try to tell yourself to simply calm down, your brain has to use immense effort, but it has almost no problem moving from fear to excitement because you are shifting from a "threat mindset" to an "opportunity mindset."

We can even choose to use fear to our advantage: find a fear that's bigger than your fear. Uncover the fear of what would happen if you didn't take action.

On that Thursday afternoon all those years ago, when my husband and I clung to each other outside a hair salon, I made the choice to allow the fear of not being able to feed our kids to circle us like a shark. I allowed it to sit uncomfortably on my shoulders every day, emboldening me to go after something bigger—something that would have normally frightened me. Fear is what convinced me that I could truly take on the challenge of owning my own business. And I allowed it to make me brave.

Some people will say that if your goals don't scare you, they aren't big enough. "Do it scared," they'll say. Let's not do it scared; let's do it bravely, excitedly. Let's accept that feeling in our stomachs like we are at the top of a roller coaster bracing ourselves for that rush of wind in our hair. Let's hold on tight and enjoy the ride.

Fear is not your enemy. In fact, fear can be your biggest ally. It can give you the push you need to shift and move toward the life you want, charging your body up and priming you for action.

LIES THAT HOLD US BACK:

- What will people think?
- This is a sign from the universe that I shouldn't try this.
- I'm too scared.
- I don't think I can do this.

TRUTHS THAT MOVE US FORWARD:

- What other people think of me is none of my business and doesn't have any bearing on my self-worth.
- I will no longer confuse comfort with safety.
- I realize being scared is normal; fear isn't a sign that I'm on the wrong path.
- When I take ownership of my fears I can do anything I put my mind to.

SPRINGBOARD: In the Interactive Reader's Guide, there is a blank Fears to Facts blueprint you can use to work through a current fear.

eight

CHOOSE TO CREATE THE TIME

Imagine yourself sitting at the kitchen table, your eyebrows furrowed while you tackle a burning issue from work. Your mind is fixated, and you've entered the state of deep work where the ideas are flowing like honey. You just need to spend another forty-five minutes mapping out the solution, and you'll be free to close your laptop and enjoy the day.

At that moment your eight-year-old comes in, bounces her soccer ball on the table, and asks if you'll go outside and play goalie. How do you respond? "Not now. I don't have the time right now," most will say. That key idea is circling in your head and you just need to get it down on paper, then later you can play.

Now imagine the same scene—you at the table in that same state of flow—when your eight-year-old comes barreling into the room holding her nose with blood pouring out between her fingers. Do you give her a quick glance and tell her, "Not now. I don't have the time"? Or do you drop everything immediately and rush to your daughter's side to tend to her?

Truth be told, you had the exact same amount of time in both situations. You just used time as your cover for the fact that you didn't want to be disturbed and didn't feel like playing soccer.* You did, however, want to stop the bloody nose and to make your child feel better. You weren't a victim of time; you used time as your excuse.

I read Dr. Gay Hendrick's description of Einstein Time, where he shared a story similar to the one I just shared with you, and it changed everything for me. Just as I hope it does for you.

I started intentionally removing the phrase "I don't have time" from my conversations. You might recall: Your words matter. And if you are telling yourself (and others) that you just don't have time, you'll eventually begin to believe it. In fact, I found that when I stopped saying that phrase, time loosened its controlling grip on me.

We have to stop being time victims and take ownership.

WHAT'S YOUR RELATIONSHIP STATUS?

We have an interesting relationship with time. If there was a spot to post our time-relationship status on social media, the line would read, "It's complicated."

There are moments we feel like we have an unlimited excess of time. We say things like, *I'll make time to do that someday.* And then just mere seconds later we'll feel the intense pressure of not having nearly enough. We say things like, *I just don't have the time to do what I need!*

It's a seesaw of emotions where we feel the push and pull of time tugging at us. We use that word *someday* to push aside our big dreams and goals because we apparently have this abundant Olympic-pool-size vault of unlimited time while simultaneously pushing those exact same dreams aside because time feels so scarce—we don't have the time to dedicate to them.

Scarcity and abundance do not apply to time. Time is simply time.

---

* By the way, let's take a minute and address the fact that it's absolutely okay to not want to play with your kid every single time they ask. It doesn't make you a bad parent that you used time as your excuse—it makes you human. It also shows your kid that Mom has interests of her own, and that's a good thing to model for your kids.

Sixty minutes on your beach vacation is exactly the same amount as sixty minutes right before your presentation to a live audience. So why do they feel so different?

The time on the beach stretches and lingers. We feel like we have ample time for a nap, reading a chapter (or two) of our book, and even savoring a fruity drink with an umbrella tucked into the straw. Those exact same sixty minutes before a presentation, though, are a sweaty, hurried mess of furiously typing and collating notes. We find ourselves glancing at the clock and discovering we're missing chunks of time. (*How has it already been thirty minutes?!*)

Those missing blocks of time are alarming, aren't they? When, unaware to you, time has been moving and you've somehow missed it. It's no surprise that we can feel life is just speeding by—we are consistently being hustled from one life event to the next. No sooner do you get in a relationship than people start asking when you'll get married. And then while you are still standing in your beautiful white gown, some guest is bound to ask when they can expect to see babies. The older we get, the faster time flies past us it seems.

It's funny when we think of the first eighteen years of our life and how they crawled by so slowly. Those last five minutes of the last day of school took at least a full year to tick by! And now, here we stand wondering where in the world time went.

Time is absolute, but the way we process and feel about time is incredibly fluid. We can bend, stretch, and even collapse time simply based on how we decide to perceive time. When we feel like we have too much to do and not enough time to do it, time streaks past. But when we slow down and intentionally choose *how* we spend our time, it stretches and unfurls like a magician's handkerchief.

IT'S NOT TIME MANAGEMENT YOU NEED

I want help with time management. It's one of the most common requests I hear from new clients and members of my program. These people are successful, but time seems like this slippery beast that controls them and keeps them hustling.

Allow me to show you behind the wizard's curtain—here's a piece of truth you won't hear from other productivity experts: *there is no time management.*

You cannot manage time. It's not an angry three-year-old throwing a tantrum in the middle of the grocery store or a wild, hairy beast tearing apart your house. It cannot be tamed or soothed; it's not out to get you and steal your energy.

You cannot manage time, but you can manage your activities. You can choose how you spend your time.

Time is never just going to appear out of nowhere. I cannot give you the extra hours in your day that you think you need to demand. You have to create the time you need out of what you have already been given. With all the inequalities of wealth in our world, time is not one of them. It's equally doled out to each of us.

It is up to us to decide how to use that time. Let go of time management and focus on your activity management instead.

Let me show you what I mean. Let's take the concept of time, which feels abstract, and make it more concrete. We think of our time like this:

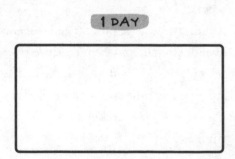

We fall into bed at night and we take a moment to think back over our day and we mentally give the day a passing or a failing grade. And let's be brutally honest here: most days we feel like we failed. We didn't do enough, we could have done more, we didn't check enough off our ridiculously long to-do list. We spend our days chasing down a thousand things, cramming the hours full with tasks and errands and chores and projects. The list goes on and on, and in reality there was no way to actually accomplish the three days' worth of tasks in one single day. We set ourselves up to fail.

Really our day is not one big, solid block of granite. It's made up of 24 hours. It looks more like this:

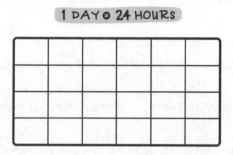

If we zoom in a bit more, we can see that we can easily break our day into smaller 15-minute blocks of time.

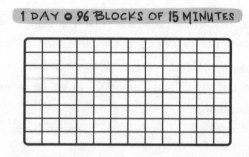

If we separate each of these 15-minute blocks, we find that our day looks like this:

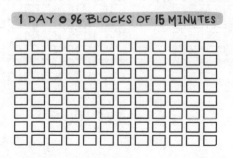

That's 96 blocks of time for you to choose your activities. There are 1,440 minutes hidden inside those 96 blocks waiting to be used in the way that you want. Yes, you. After all, if you don't have ownership over your own time, who does?

Reflect back on that opening story for this chapter and your responses to your fictitious child. You are not a victim of time; you are the boss of time.

We know we cannot manage time, but we can choose to manage the activities in the time we have. There are four ways you can spend this time:

Resting · Doing · Distracting · Thinking

Let's dive into each of these so we can begin to choose how our time will bend.

Resting

Resting might seem like a strange place to begin, but rest is one of the most important things we can gift ourselves to achieve the success we crave. We mistakenly believe that if we follow the *hustle mantra* we'll find success, so we are afraid to stop moving. But we cannot exhale if we do not take time to inhale.

Our bodies require rest, so we need to begin by allotting 32 of our blocks to sleeping.

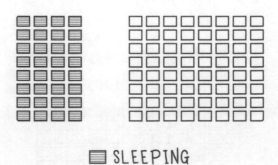

▤ SLEEPING

We *cannot*

EXHALE

if we do not *take time* to

INHALE.

I know that right now you might be disappointed that you are already seeing time disappear, and you might even try to fool yourself into thinking you don't really need 8 hours of sleep . . . maybe you can skate by with less. Sure, you can do that—you can steal some time, but you'll be ineffective. If you've ever had a night with only 4 hours of sleep thanks to a cranky child or a cranky term paper, you might remember you aren't exactly your best self when you don't get enough sleep. Your quality of work drops down as much as 30 percent, and you aren't the brightest little ray of sunshine to everyone around you.

Healthy adults need anywhere between 7 and 9 hours of sleep. Acknowledge it, accept it, and move on. Sleep is a nonnegotiable. Keep in mind we still have 64 glorious blocks of untapped potential we can use. But even with those 64 blocks, we don't want to constantly be in action.

We falsely believe that to be productive our blocks should be filled with *doing* and should look like this:

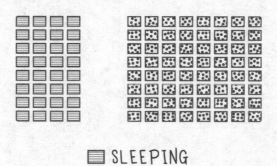

Truth be told, you can expect to see all four categories scattered throughout your day, including *resting* and *distracting.** That might surprise you—we'll get to *distracting* in just a moment, but for now, let's focus on *resting.* No different from when you work out in the gym and need a

---

* I have a feeling you'd like me to share a graphic that tells you exactly how many blocks you should spend on each activity. I could tell you what I think are the perfect percentages of time that should be spent on each, but those are my percentages—not yours. You need to decide how you want to spend your time. After all, you own your time, I don't.

moment to bring down your heart rate and gulp down some air, your brain needs rest too.

Pockets of rest can include meditation, closing your eyes and taking a break away from the computer, naps, or simply sitting quietly outside and watching the rest of the world hurry by for a few minutes. Resting moments are anything that feels renewing and restorative both physically and mentally.

Doing

I cannot possibly find the time. How many times a day do you think you tell yourself that? Your time feels "thin . . . like butter that has been scraped over too much bread."* The question is, Which one is the problem: not enough butter or too much bread?

There's a limited amount of butter, so the obvious answer is there's way too much bread on the plate. We can keep scraping the butter, or we can choose to slather it on the best pieces of bread.

We know our day is already filled with *doing*, but what exactly is it we are doing? Are we using our time (our butter) the way we really want?

Let me drop a heart-stopping truth for you: we do have the time. We've hidden behind the excuse of not having enough instead of taking a good, hard look at our bread to see what needs to be taken off the plate.

When we use the phrase "I don't have the time," we are lying to ourselves. We are simply choosing to not prioritize whatever it is that truly needs the space.

For me, I've replaced that phrase with "I don't *want* to give this my time" or "That's not a priority for me right now." This makes it easier to step back and acknowledge that the way my day is spent is, ultimately, my choice. Time doesn't demand how I spend it—I do.

Sometimes, though, we can have difficulty prioritizing the tasks we really want to work on because we are busy *doing* for everybody else—filling everyone else's needs but our own. We tuck our own goals and dreams away because we think that's what we are supposed to do.

---

* Quick hat tip to my fellow Tolkien nerds out there who recognize this Bilbo Baggins quote.

This was the trap Donna Sava, an alumna of my program, fell into with her kids. Donna is an incredibly smart and creative woman who produces children's books and animated feature films. She has twin teenage boys she adores, who kept her running from one activity to the next, making her feel like she was in a haze. As she put it, her afternoons were "a hot mess." But she was following the Good Mom Rule—the one that says: good moms say yes to everything their kids want to do.*

"If it's something for school or one of my kids, I don't want to say no because I want to be there for [them], but at the same time, I'm looking at my watch going, 'How am I going to be here and there?'" she confided.

Donna and I dove deeper into this, and she said, "I think that's the biggest struggle—I want to do it all, but I can't do it all." Because she was seeing her actions as a way to pour love into her kids, it was hard to prioritize anything else. She and I came up with a plan to sit down and talk with her family and prioritize the activities together.

When I mentioned this strategy, the relief could be heard in her voice. "I haven't really even asked them. . . . If I'm going to put this much time in, where would [they] rather me spend my time [with them]?"

She was excited to call a meeting that very weekend to talk it out with her family. Less than one year after Donna and I worked through this stumbling block, her animated film debuted on Netflix in the top 5, which shows me that Donna found a way to slather a lot more butter on her bread.

When it comes to *doing*, you do not have to do it all, and you don't always have to sacrifice time on your tasks for the sake of others. Your goals and dreams are no less significant than anyone else's—including your kids'.

Distracting

Many of the tasks that eat away at our time are really just distractions, pulling us away from our true priorities. Distractions can take many

---

* The mom guilt is real. The day our babies are born, they hand us over that beautiful bundle along with a nice, little package of mom guilt. And by nice, little package, I mean a big, heaping package. It's so heavy, it's falling out of the wrapping.

different forms: scrolling social media; mindlessly playing a game; even the committees, projects, and obligations we have said yes to over the years that are no longer aligned with how we want to spend our time—all of those are distractions.

When we give ourselves permission to let go of the things that no longer serve us, we gain an opportunity to pursue what is aligned with our purpose. For the committees and projects that you feel guilty quitting, think about your decision to quit not as a failure but as an intentional strategy.

Sometimes it's not a big leap of faith we need; it's a stopping point of faith. Quitting is not an end—it's the first step in refocusing and redefining your life. It allows you to reclaim lost time and is the biggest ally in making time bend to your will.

Here's an interesting twist, though—we actually do need to have some distractions in our day.* You might be surprised to read that, but here's what you have to keep in mind: We need to make time for play. We overcomplicate our relationship with time because we worry that if we aren't constantly hustling forward toward some tangible goal, we aren't doing anything worthwhile.

Play is essential for our brains, but we tend to undervalue it because it seems silly. We beat ourselves up for wasting time when we could have spent it being "productive." What's ironic, though, is that by giving ourselves space to enjoy time, we become *more* productive. When more frequent play is incorporated into our days, we see dramatic increases in creativity, attention, and performance.

We want to get rid of the distractions that pull at us and make us feel guilty but allow space and room for the distractions that benefit us.

I had a conversation not long ago with Tyanna Smith, a member of my program who was struggling to find time in her day to work on her business.

With her husband back in school and a two-year-old at home, she

---

* Let's take note of that very important word—*some*—written here. Not a lot of distractions . . . some.

was doing her best to make growing her business a priority, but it wasn't easy. As someone who started my own first business with two little kids playing at my feet, I understand that struggle. Tyanna told me she wants to "find the satisfaction in the day-to-day, so that I truly am happy with what I'm doing."

I encouraged her to look at the many tiny pockets of time scattered throughout her day, bank them up, and combine them to give her a few bigger blocks of time. (This is one of my favorite ways to stretch time.) One place I wanted her to look was at her distractions—could she get rid of some of the activities that weren't really helping her?

We all have little things that we do, or that we find ourselves doing, whether that's scrolling on our phone or watching a TV show or just mindlessly doing something. We don't think about these little activities we've built into our lives, but we tend to lump them together as "time wasters." But not every distraction is a time waster, and learning how to spot which ones we need to get rid of and which ones we need to keep is incredibly simple.

Give yourself a quick check-in. Step back and notice: Is this distraction nourishing or negative? Is it something that's good for me and allows me to catch my breath, or is it something that keeps me from finding that satisfaction Tyanna mentioned earlier? You can search for lists of time wasters (it's actually a question I get asked all the time), but here's the secret: only you can decide if an activity is nourishing or negative.

You just have to stop and ask yourself the question, *How do I feel after I finish this?*

If you binge three episodes of your favorite show back-to-back, it could be negative or it could be nourishing. Ask yourself the question and then listen for your own answer. When you've finished your mini binge-watching session, do you feel good and satisfied? Or do you feel sluggish and irritated? Life is a choose-your-own-adventure story, so choose.

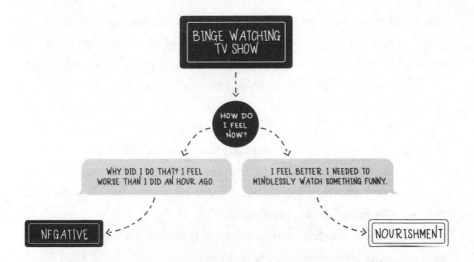

If you flip off the TV and think, *That was just what I needed. I needed that space to just mindlessly watch something funny*, that's nourishment.

But if you think to yourself, *Agh, I feel worse about myself than I did an hour ago*—congratulations, you've just discovered a time waster. Let's jettison that activity and create time for something else—something that *is* nourishing.

This same practice holds true when thinking about quitting those bigger distractions. Use this practice to help you decide if the tasks and projects you've said yes to in the past still align.

It really is that simple. As Tyanna shared with me, "I think it takes . . . making [how I spend time] a priority. . . . It's about making that choice." She's absolutely right.

Thinking

Too often we confuse activity with achievement. Yes, we need action, but action doesn't always have to look like *doing*. Sometimes activity needs to be the quiet, still act of deep thought and application. We have a tendency, though, to bind our feelings of self-worth tightly to our daily achievements. We need to loosen those knots.

This is a mindset shift, and there are times when writing this very book that I had to remind myself of this. Writing a book requires giant blocks of time. If I had tied my achievement to how many words I typed during each of my blocks, I would have ended more days feeling disappointed than inspired.

Writing this book meant sometimes sitting on my screened porch staring off at the mountains while I untangled the tentacles of ideas that were swirling in my brain. At other times it meant walking in circles through the house muttering to myself like Sherlock Holmes as I tediously unlocked a concept.* Some days I didn't type a single word, but that didn't mean I wasn't getting closer to my achievement—the fact that you hold this book in your hands is proof of that.

Thinking is the foundation for all action, but we need to stop and actually think about what we are thinking.

Every day we have over 6,200 thoughts, which, roughly calculated, means we have about four new thoughts every single minute. Here's the big question, though: What are we thinking about?

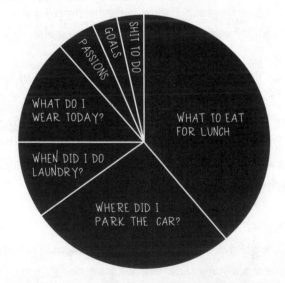

With our brain being bombarded with thoughts every second of the day, we need to make sure we are gifting time to the big thoughts like our Cathedral. Instead we get tripped up in the triviality of life. We allow stress

---

* Truthfully, it was more like Professor Trelawney most of the time.

ON PURPOSE

and anxiety to set up permanent camp in our brain, stealing away precious space in our thinking.

Dana Autry expressed this very thing with me on a live group coaching call. She shared, "I'm dealing with overwhelm and fatigue like never before. I try to prioritize, but it seems like there's so much outside my control. How do you move forward when it feels like you're barely treading water?"

I asked the other women on the call to hold up their hand if they've ever felt that way. Every single one sheepishly raised their arms. We all know that feeling—trying to make everything above the surface look calm and together, but underneath the water we are fiercely kicking our legs nonstop. We are exhausting ourselves. It's no wonder our brains are worn out and we feel brain-dead at the end of the day.

When it comes to our tasks, we need to take the thinking out of it wherever we can. Your brain is already processing insane amounts of information, so let's choose which thoughts to process—and let's choose to get rid of the trivial. We can silo the stress and allow space for the thoughts that will help us truly step into what we want.

When I explained this idea of siloing stress to Dana, I shared with her how I was using this strategy myself. While I've been writing this book, we've also been dealing with the college application process with Jack. (Talk about stressful!) And while college applications themselves are not trivial, the stress and extra thinking that come with the applications definitely are. I was finding that I was worrying away entire blocks of writing time wondering if Jack had done his college research or if he had looked into taking a test prep course.

I was stressed. John was stressed. And, let's be honest, we were stressing Jack out at the same time. We made a family decision to "silo the stress" by assigning Thursday nights as our college planning nights. Thursday evenings after dinner, the three of us would sit on the couch and check in on Jack and hold him accountable. The rest of the week, the topic was completely off limits—no talking about applications, no worrying about essays, and no interrogations on his progress.

I can't tell you how freeing it was for all three of us. Because we were checking in once a week, if thoughts popped into my head on a Monday, I simply jotted down a note in my planner knowing I would circle around on that Thursday night. My brain space was free to focus on my writing.*

We get caught up in the nitpicky details of life and lose sight of the big picture. We spend an excessive amount of time on the things that don't really require it: the worrying, the stress, the tweaking and reworking of tasks and projects that don't really need it. We lose time struggling to make life perfect. It's no wonder we are overwhelmed and feel there's not enough time in the day. We are spending a disproportionate amount of time thinking about the minutia—the unimportant.

Spending an hour choosing just the right font for a presentation or working endlessly to keep the house immaculately clean and ultraorganized so it is no longer a home but more like a catalog shoot—these are pulls at our time that we can relinquish. When we give ourselves containers to limit how long those tasks should take, we free up massive amounts of time and brain space.

There are an incredible amount of things in our world we cannot control. If we took the time to list them all out, we would find that we would need a sheet of paper the size of a football field. Our list of what we can control is small, but it is mighty. We can choose our thoughts. When you choose your thoughts, you control your time.

THERE'S A LOT TO LIFE

I want to double my monthly revenue.

Jenny Johnson shared her big goal with me during a group coaching call. Jenny is an amazing woman running a business with a lot of heart

---

* Side bonus: Jack stepped up and took a bigger role in his own path to college. It helps that Mom stopped with the surprise cross-examinations.

behind it—her concierge nursing company focuses on helping seniors live happily into their golden years.

Together we mapped out how to make her goal a reality, and once she could see the milestones to focus on, I could tell she was feeling like success was within reach. And then a cloud passed over her face.

"But here is the kicker," she confided. "I also want to run a half-marathon later this year, I homeschool my kids, and I have a marriage I need to water. . . . There's a lot to life."

Understatement of the year, right there. There's not a lot—there's an absolute ton. And if we are caught up in the idea of balance, there's no way to water all the areas of life.

You see, magic doesn't happen when life is centered and balanced—it happens when we lean into a priority. When we start focusing on a priority, we will go out of balance—giving it more time over other items. The challenge is not finding balance—it's counterbalancing. It's shifting our focus and spending our time where it makes the most impact in our day and then shifting it back. That's where harmony comes in.

We have to be willing to go out of balance, but this can feel scary because we like the false feeling of safety balance brings.

We scramble to try and make everything feel even. We don't concentrate our time in the one direction we really want to go; we thin it out and spread it around (like our butter scraped on too much bread). In chasing this illusion of balance, we end up creating a life that feels busy—not meaningful. We have to be willing to be out-of-balance. We need to be willing to not do everything. That's the real magic.

I reminded Jenny, "You are more than a business owner or a person who runs half-marathons. You're more than a wife or a homeschooling mom." Every facet of your life needs watering. We don't just want to pour everything in at work, but we cannot fully pour ourselves into everything all at once either.

I shared with her a framework I created called the Goal Setting Matrix, which gives a bird's-eye view of your year. The point of this framework is to allow you to find that harmony.

	JAN	FEB	MAR	APR	MAY	JUN	JUL	AUG	SEP	OCT	NOV	DEC
PERSONAL												
HOME												
WORK												

"You see," I told Jenny, "we cannot water all our goals at the same time. If you are going to focus on your revenue goal, you have to lift up on the watering can a little bit in those other areas. Then once you feel like this is in a rhythm, maybe . . . when we get to the end of the three-month period, then you can shift and give the half-marathon a little more time. That's not to say you're not getting in shape for your half-marathon now; it's just that it's not as big of a focus.

"Then in the months leading up to your race, when you are frequently running longer distances, it's going to need more of your time. You'll need to pour a little less water on your work goals."

Using the Goal Setting Matrix, you can see a bird's-eye view of what's happening for each of your goals. This allows you to choose which times of the year you want to pour more into each area of your life.

JENNY'S GOAL SETTING MATRIX

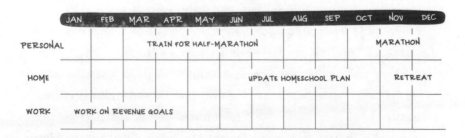

	JAN	FEB	MAR	APR	MAY	JUN	JUL	AUG	SEP	OCT	NOV	DEC
PERSONAL			TRAIN FOR HALF-MARATHON								MARATHON	
HOME							UPDATE HOMESCHOOL PLAN				RETREAT	
WORK	WORK ON REVENUE GOALS											

Marriages and relationships need constant watering, but we can set some practices in place to make sure our marriages get the constant attention they deserve. Regular date nights and little rituals that help keep the fires going are really important without feeling like the relationship is on autopilot. For the past seventeen years, John and I have had a Sunday evening ritual. As soon as the kids go to bed, he and I have an at-home date night—sometimes it's a movie, or it might be sitting on the porch sipping cocktails and chatting.

We made it a point to explain to our kids when they were very young that our marriage is the foundation for our family—it needs love and attention just like they do. And because we prioritized it, our kids did too. Sunday bedtimes were not the night for extra glasses of water or longer stories—it was never an argument because it was never up for negotiation.*

I could call our Sunday nights a habit, but I prefer to call it a lifestyle. I'm not worried about carving out time for my marriage. I've already taken the stress of time away, which allows me to be *all in* on my marriage in the moment.

Jenny made the decision to do less and focus her time. By letting go of balance she shared, "I just feel so good . . . and accomplished. I am feeling much more valuable to myself and to my family." That's what bending time is all about.

WAIT, WHERE AM I?

Have you ever driven your car on the highway and suddenly realized you don't remember the last few miles? It's like you suddenly come to, only to realize that even though you were driving safely, time somehow slipped past?

Driving can easily run on autopilot for us—the pressure on the pedals, how much to turn the steering wheel—we don't have to think about it. But when you were sixteen and learning to drive, you had to focus on each little part of driving. I know this, having recently taught a teenager

---

* Funny enough, as our kids got older, they would defend that time for us and make sure it remained protected if there were activities or events that might run late on Sundays.

to drive and spending an entire afternoon experiencing the learning curve of finding the appropriate amount of pressure to apply to the brakes! My neck will attest, it's not an easy skill.

Jack has to focus on each little moving part, so he's much more aware and engaged. When I drive, and when you drive, you likely don't have to think about each thing. We give in to the road hypnosis . . . and we often give in to life hypnosis as well.

Are you spending your days on autopilot? Slipping into the motions of the everyday? We want to break the reverie and slow time down. It's not time management; it's savoring the moments. Slowing down and being present: that's what allows us to bend, stretch, and contort time to our will.

You've probably noticed a recurring theme throughout this chapter— it's not the action that matters, it's the intention behind it. We want to invest in ourselves. We don't just want to find ourselves doing or thinking; we want to choose to think and do what's most important. That's what allows us to feel ready for the curves in the road that life will throw at us.

But we'll be tackling that next.

LIES THAT HOLD US BACK:

- I don't have enough time.
- There's too much to do.
- I'll do it someday when I have more time.
- Time is just moving too fast.

TRUTHS THAT MOVE US FORWARD:

- If I want more time, I have to decide how I spend the time I already have.
- I give myself permission to let go of the things that no longer serve me so that I can pursue what is aligned with my purpose.
- If something is a priority, I won't put it off for Someday.
- I can be present in my own life by mindfully choosing my activities.

SPRINGBOARD: Resting is an important activity we often overlook. Brainstorm a few ideas for small moments you can incorporate into your daily routine to renew and recharge.

part four

ALTERATION

Answers the Question: What If?

CHOOSE TO GIVE GRACE

My eyes frantically scurried across the grainy black-and-white screen, desperate to see movement.

Just minutes before, I had burst through the doors of my obstetrician's office wild-eyed and in an absolute panic. The nurse had immediately hustled me past all of the patiently waiting women and into the dark room where I now lay propped up on my elbows feverishly scanning the ultrasound.

And suddenly there she was.

Like the wings of a hummingbird, her little heartbeat flickered onto the screen as my elbows gave way and released my back against the thin, crinkly paper covering the table. Little rivers of salt burned at the edges of my eyes and snaked their way down into my ears. I was so busy reveling in my relief that I missed the serious look on the nurse's face as she quietly stood up and left the room to bring in my doctor.

The rest of my time in that little dark room feels oddly both crystal clear and hideously warped. The words my doctor spoke next sounded as if she were underwater, distorted and slurred, but I can still repeat them word for word today. She gently told me that Baby Girl, with the heartbeat like hummingbird wings, wouldn't survive longer than a few more days. There was nothing we could do but wait for those wings to stop beating and allow her to slip gracefully into heaven.

I don't know what it feels like to drown, but I can only imagine that it maybe feels similar to what I felt lying on that thin white paper—gulping for air, silently begging for someone to pull me up and out of that room. But no one could save me.

I spent the next three days hoping for a miracle. On day four, I woke up to Jack jumping into my bed, throwing his little body toward me in a hug with the biggest grin on his face. He couldn't wait to wish me a Happy Mother's Day and present me with the teacup with a tiny little sprout he had planted inside it. I did my best to feign excitement and grit my teeth into a smile because I knew he had no way of understanding that waves of pain were just starting to barrel through my body.

While Jack spent the entire holiday parked in front of the TV watching an endless loop of cartoons, John and I sat on the hard bathroom floor as we lost her and cried until our eyes were ringed red and we could barely breathe.

In the late afternoon, John ran me a bath and left me alone for the first time all day. I sat in the tub, with my arms curled around my knees, letting the hot anger and sadness freely run out of my eyes and into the water when I felt a sudden, noticeable shift.

God came and saw me that day. He and I hadn't spoken for quite some time at that point, but He hadn't forgotten me. I had begged in the dark room for someone to lift me up and out, and here He was, lifting me out of that water I was drowning in and pulling me up for air.

He spoke of redemption and He spoke of anger and how the choice was mine. The paths were there for me—and me alone—to choose. To find purpose in this pain or to let the hot anger swallow me whole. It was tempting to choose anger; this, after all, was not supposed to be part of the plan. But knowing that there was a choice somehow made it easier.

At the time I didn't know I would start a business and I had no idea I would one day write books, but I knew that day that I had been shown a gift. It was the first time I truly understood the power of choice and I knew my purpose was steeped in it. It's certainly not the path I had planned to take—my map had looked smoother and less bumpy—but it's the detour that has led me to my true life. I like to believe that dark room filled with sadness has brought me to who I am now.

That's not an easy choice, but it's the choice I have to make.

Over the past few weeks, John and I have sat and had more than a thousand conversations about sharing this story. It is, without question, the darkest day of our marriage. To share something so personal that, years later, the wounds still feel fresh and raw is not something I wanted to do without talking with him. But here we are—together—finding the purpose in that pain.

Plans get derailed—even the best-laid ones don't always work out. We always have a choice when this happens: we can stress about the plans or we can keep moving forward—one foot in front of the other—even when it's hard.

We feel uncertain of what to do because we are no longer anywhere on that map we've made, and we worry we are wandering in circles. But we aren't really lost. We just need to reorient ourselves. And we can do that using three A's:

Acknowledge · Assess · Adjust

ACKNOWLEDGE

Whether you call it the Universe or Source or the Divine or God, we've probably all felt at some point in our lives that there was some force conspiring against us—throwing obstacles into our paths and laying destruction in our plans.

As a planner, preparer, and doer we feel like it should all be mapped out perfectly. The problem is, we have a tendency to over-romanticize the path, so we are disappointed when it doesn't go exactly as we imagine it in our heads.

We get so caught up in the goal that sometimes we become blind to the opportunities that come—not from the goal itself, but from the diverted path. We convince ourselves that getting off the track means we have failed, so we plunge our heads in the sand and pretend that everything is okay.

Acknowledging is not acceptance; it's awareness. It's recognizing that things aren't going as planned because life tends to throw in a monkey wrench from time to time. If you were to truly map out how good planning works, it would look like this:

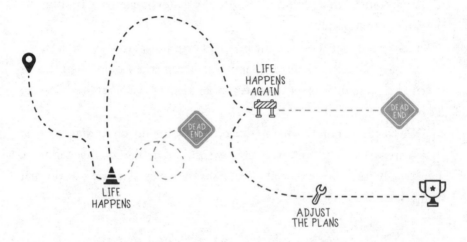

Getting off the path doesn't mean we have failed; it just means our path isn't straight. Here's the catch: It's never straight. It's full of twists and turns. Sometimes these roadblocks are really the detours that get us to the life we are meant to be living.

We take needless pride in fighting through the muck instead of stepping back and realizing we just need to take a deep breath and look around to see where we've gotten off the path. Your brain stubbornly wants to stay on the same path because it feels safe. It likes the well-worn path because it has kept you alive—even if you aren't *really* living. Acknowledging that isn't always easy, but it's always the first step. Stand in the seat of your own power and accept that there may have been mistakes made or issues ignored. That's now firmly in the past because you are now ready to get back to moving forward.

ASSESS

Once you've taken a chance to acknowledge, it's time to assess. Let's rephrase that—assess without judgment. Retrace your steps and backtrack to find where you got off the trail. When you are lost in the middle of the forest, you cannot see the right path—and we already know you'll be traveling in circles if you just start wandering—so take a step back. Walk away for a day or two, allowing your bruised ego to heal and giving your brain a chance to stop berating you nonstop about how you have failed.

Spend a little time with some nourishing distractions: watch videos where people make fools of themselves, or knit a scarf for your dog, or learn to play "Hot Cross Buns" on your kid's recorder. Anything that will allow you (and your brain) some space away from the problem. While writing this book, there were more than a few times I found myself straying off track. When I discovered myself feeling lost and at the dead end known as writer's block, I thoroughly deep cleaned the fridge, twice; I taught myself how to make ramen from scratch (yes, noodles, broth, eggs, the whole bit); and I recaulked the shower.*

Give yourself a container of time to just breathe a bit. The word *container* here is a big one, so don't read too fast and skip over it. Yes, you need to go and goof off for a bit—but within a container. A container of time has a start time and it has a set end time. We don't want to wander too far into the dark catacombs of distraction.

We want to intentionally step away so we can come back with fresh

---

* A more complete list of my nourishing distractions could include: turning on eighties music and loudly mangling all the lyrics while my kids pretended to not be embarrassed by my singing, rewatching the full *Lord of the Rings* series back-to-back-to-back-to—you get the idea—and finishing a one-thousand-piece puzzle in a single afternoon. Now you know all my book-writing secrets.

eyes and a fresh mindset. When we are too busy picking apart our mistakes, we can't find the clarity we need.

We simply need to retrace our breadcrumbs and find where we got diverted.

It's Time to Check In

The most obvious place to look is your check-in system. Hands down, I find that this is the biggest pitfall that causes people to get off track. One of my clients, Andrea Mazur, discovered that in the busyness of everyday life, she had skipped two months of working on her goals. She had already done the first step—she acknowledged that her plans had gone off the rails—but she wasn't going to let that keep her from seeing them through.

On one of our live calls, she asked me, "What's the best strategy to revisit goals regularly? I feel like I need a better check-in or tracking system." Immediately the other women on the call started typing in the chat, chiming in that this was a struggle for them as well.

This is what I love about having these types of open conversations with groups of women—we start to realize we aren't alone in our struggles. Instead of feeling called out, you can begin to feel called in—into a circle of women who are really there to support you, who see you and love you, imperfections and all. (Because we all have them.)

So, if this is you—if you are someone who feels like you continually start goals with a fire in your belly only to find that all you have left is a smoldering pile of ash a few months (or even weeks) later, you are not alone. There's nothing wrong with you; we just need to assess the way you are checking in—*or* if you are checking in at all.

The first question we need to ask ourselves is, Is this goal still for me? Sometimes we set ourselves up with a lofty goal in January only to find that we get to June and we've got no gas left in the tank because we don't truly love this goal. We think we are supposed to stick with it, though, because winners never quit. Listen, *quit happens*. And that's a good thing. You are not married to your goals. I used to tell people, "Plans are written in pencil, goals are written in ink." Oh, what a fool I was.

Erase those goals that no longer align and leave the guilt in those eraser shavings. There's no shame in trying something out only to realize it's not for you. Remember, only those who never try are the ones who are failing. Leaving a goal (or two) in the dust behind you doesn't make you a failure; it makes you a beautiful work in progress.

If, though, in asking that question, you find the goal is still for you but it's been a little neglected, then let's find a way to bring it forward into the light. If we want to live an *On Purpose* life, we want the joy to be found in our everydays. It's not the crossing of that finish line that brings us happiness; it's the in-between moments where we are consistently making progress. Small daily progress is the biggest secret to slipping into bed each night feeling satisfied and fulfilled, so we need to find a touchpoint with our goals each day.

Listen, you already have a lot on your plate, so let's make it simple to do a quick assessment. That way you always feel that forward momentum, which means you always feel satisfied with what you are doing each day.

Have You Lost Sight of Your Vision?

Let's start with a simple assessment that might make you laugh because it's so easy: vision boards. I told you it would make you laugh or maybe even roll your eyes. Vision boards are not a new concept by any stretch of the imagination, but—here's the catch—most people fail to use them in a way that truly benefits them.*

Have you ever left a coffee cup sitting on your dresser or side table for just a minute or two? You set it down, with every intention of coming back to it, but you walk away and promptly forget all about it. Then three days later you discover the science experiment that once was your coffee and wonder how you didn't notice it until that very moment. You've walked past that spot a thousand times and just didn't register it was there. The same thing happens to vision boards.

---

* My favorite way to make a vision board is to gather a group of women to dream of their futures and create their boards together. All you need is a stack of magazines, good appetizers, and drinks . . . the party brings itself.

Many women dutifully spend the start of the new year creating their board for the year, which they then tuck away on a shelf or hang in an out-of-the-way spot—where it's promptly forgotten. Those goals are literally (and figuratively) gathering dust, so it's no surprise they get abandoned.

Several years ago, I began hanging my own vision board in my closet. I get dressed every single day, so while I'm picking out my clothes (or rather, stressing about what I'm going to wear), I take a quick look at my board and decide what I'm going to do that very day to get me closer to my vision. That helps spur some action.

The key, though, which most people don't realize, is that you need to move the vision board around. For me, in my closet I switch it up *at least* every quarter. It will start off in January hanging next to my shoes, then by April it might be next to the tank tops on the shelf, then in September it can be found above my full-length mirror. It's a Where's Waldo of vision boards because it's never in the same place for too long. That helps it stay fresh and not blend in with the background like that old cup of coffee.

I didn't always have a nice-sized closet, so instead I would move it to my bathroom and then over to the spot where my makeup was stored—all places I go every day. Essentially what I have done is create a visual daily reflection simply by building off an existing habit. I already have a habit of getting dressed every morning, so I piggyback off that to make sure I'm doing a quick daily check-in.

We could call this habit stacking because that's what it really is—taking an activity you already do and tying in a new habit to follow. If we were to write this as a formula it would look like this:

Before/After _____, **I Will** _____
                    Existing Habit   **New Habit**

In my example, we could phrase it like this: After I pick out my clothes, I will check in on my goals.

When it comes to making sure that we're staying on track, we can use habit stacking in a thousand different ways. For example, I already have a big family meeting on the last Sunday of every month, so I habit stacked it and started focusing on each family member's goals at the start of that meeting. We review the past month's goals and decide what we each want to work on for the coming month. This has the side bonus of keeping us all accountable for one another.

If you have a monthly habit, like paying your gym membership or reconciling your bank account, piggyback off these activities and add in a monthly check-in where you ask yourself a few questions:

- *Does this goal still align with what I want?*
  - Is it time to burn this goal to the ground and start something fresh or do you still love this goal?
- *Am I on track with where I want to be?*
  - Not where you think you are *supposed* to be, but where you realistically want to be. Are you still moving forward? Do you need to adjust your expectations?
- *If I'm not, what's happening to pull me from my path?*
  - What are the excuses you are using to keep from working on this? Are you hiding behind a story that you tell yourself? Are you needing to make more time? Do you need to call in someone else to help as an accountability partner?
- *What do I want to focus on this month?*
  - This is a great opportunity to take a look at your Goal Setting Matrix that we discussed in the last chapter to see if your goal needs any readjustment or if it's time to shift your focus toward another area of your life.
- *What new habits do I want to cultivate that will help me get closer to my goal?*
  - Remember the idea of building self-trust we discussed back in chapter 6? We want to establish new breadcrumbs—a pattern of following through and trusting ourselves. Small habits build up and bring you the identity you want, so what are the habits you want to cultivate this month that will help you accomplish your goal?

The key with assessment is that we don't have to wait until we've lost our way. We can choose to intentionally stop and question our progress regularly so that we don't ever have to find ourselves feeling discombobulated and disoriented. By creating a system of checking in periodically, you can easily see your wins and use them as springboards to keep the momentum going. And you can see where you are stumbling and create a detour, which we will talk about in just a moment.

What I want to encourage you to do is constantly question, consistently prod and look at how you are living. Does it feel intentional and soul-filling or does it feel like you are simply going through the motions, checking the boxes of what life has handed you? Has your life turned into a series of tomorrows or are you living each day to its fullest?

Taking 2 minutes a day and about 20 minutes a month to simply look at how you are living is truly an investment in yourself. That's about 16 hours out of the 8,760 you are gifted every year. Stop, acknowledge, and assess, and then it's time to adjust.

ADJUST

Life is filled with constant adjustments. Sometimes it's minor tweaks and other times it's creating a whole new separate path for yourself. Adjusting isn't failing—it's allowing the flexibility that life requires. There's a reason why architects create buildings and bridges to bend and move with the wind. That flexibility is what ultimately makes them able to withstand whatever comes their way. Whether it's hurricane winds or earthquakes, they will continue to stand strong and true thanks to their flexibility.

It may not be high winds we need to withstand, but the earthquakes of daily life definitely require some flexibility.

Taska Sanford is a woman with a quick wit and an easy smile. As one of my alumnae, I have a soft spot for her because I have had the opportunity to watch her establish and grow her company from the ground up.

Her purpose is woven throughout the fibers of her business—connecting kids and families with nature through art and science. As a solopreneur she built up some great wins, and then life gave her an earthquake—her mom fell ill and Taska needed to step into the role of primary caregiver.

She shared with me, "My entire business . . . has been really derailed, and I don't know what to do to regain some momentum. . . . I was really in the groove . . . but as soon as things like doctor visits and tests came up, it just sort of fell apart."

Taska had gone from full throttle, leaning heavily into work, to pulling the emergency brake and skidding like a rally car into a new role of primary caregiver. Caring for her mom required at least three-quarters of her time, leaving only about one-quarter to split between work and a personal life. It's no wonder she was feeling burned out, exhausted, and like she had totally lost her way.

Suddenly her priorities had shifted dramatically. Growing her business was no longer the top priority; her mom (rightly) had taken its place. We touched on this idea in the last chapter when we talked about letting go of balance. When we want to see growth or improvement, we have to lean more heavily into a single area of our life, but we also need to counterbalance. There is a reshuffling of priorities that needs to happen. Sometimes it's intentional and planned, and other times life springs it on us like a jump scare in a horror movie, causing us to scatter our popcorn everywhere, leaving us feeling shellshocked and disoriented.

"I don't know what I should be doing day-to-day in this mixed role," Taska admitted, defeated. "And I don't even know what success looks like at this point." She and I chatted about how difficult it feels to get anything done, especially when it seems like you have 10 million things to accomplish. When you are an entrepreneur, it can easily feel like you wear all the hats if you aren't careful.

I suggested to Taska that since her mom was the main priority and we couldn't control times for doctor visits and medications, we needed to focus on what she could control—how she ran her business. Essentially we went through and acknowledged that things needed to change, then we assessed and decided together that the focus of her business time should be on growth. Now it was time to make the adjustments needed.

I recommended that she list out all the tasks that she was currently including in her job description and then pull out a pair of scissors and start cutting it down, removing as many of the non–growth-related tasks as possible. We temporarily moved tasks, like new product development and innovations, from her job description and instead focused her limited time on marketing and finance.

I advised her, "While innovation might be a part of your business you really enjoy, right now we have to see that as an *extra*. We want to focus on what makes the biggest impact for the growth right now. And then let's look for things you can possibly batch or group together so that when you do have your little sliver of work time, you can use it as a deeper dive. For example, maybe you do all the marketing tasks on Monday. That way, you get in that marketing mindset and your brain is able to get into that flow, where you can do deeper work and it's not as taxing."

"Oh, that makes so much more sense," Taska said, sounding relieved. "I actually was [doing] the opposite . . . scratch[ing] the surface. . . . I think actually hearing you say to use those pockets so I could do a deeper dive . . . sounds way more rewarding."

"This is a temporary adjustment to get us through the time crunch," I reminded Taska. "Then we can circle back and adjust again in six months. At that point, we can add back in some of the other tasks that aren't growth-focused."

Making an adjustment can be like a detour—a temporary rerouting off your path—until you are able to get back to the main road. And then there are other times when the adjustment isn't temporary at all.

IS IT THE SITUATION OR IS IT YOU?

"Breast cancer is one of the best things that happened to me."

When Kimberly Gerber said those words, I remember being midsip from my water bottle and almost choking. They stopped me short. I unfortunately know a good number of women who have fought breast cancer, all them brave warriors, but I don't think I know any who have made such a bold statement about it before.

Kimberly is president of a corporate training company for leadership communication; she is a powerhouse woman. At the age of forty-three, her life seemed all together and perfectly mapped out for success. She was growing a thriving business, raising three small kids, and running triathlons on the weekends. "On the outside you wouldn't look at me and think anything was wrong," she admitted. "I didn't, except I was dead tired all the time. And so when I got the cancer diagnosis, I thought, *That makes sense.*"

It was a wake-up call that life on autopilot with a jam-packed calendar and no boundaries needed to make a dramatic shift. Stress had stealthily set up a permanent home without Kimberly ever really realizing it was living there. Her days were filled with the financial stress of running a business in a downturn economy, toxic clients she didn't enjoy working with, relational tension with former friends, and even physical strain from working to reclaim her fitness after becoming a mother.

After allowing some time for her diagnosis to sink in, Kimberly decided to make some drastic changes in her life. She got out what she calls her pink permission slips—permission to graduate clients who really just added toxic stress in her life, permission to do less, permission to make the hard decisions without the guilt. She cut her client base down significantly by focusing solely on her ideal clients. She reached out and got help from her amazing network of friends and family, who showed up in droves for her, filling her fridge with six months' worth of food, and she flexed her *no* muscle more often.

"The pink permission slip was a really powerful tool I used through the whole thing. If I didn't want to do something, I would ask myself, 'Do I need to pull out a permission slip?' The funny thing was, it really was just for me—I didn't need to explain that I had cancer to most people—I just needed to use it to set my boundaries in my own mind."

It's time to *stop compromising* with

YOURSELF.

That's the funny thing—the permission slips are for no one but yourself. You don't need permission to go out and get the life you want . . . you have to decide to give yourself permission. No one else can do that for you.

It's time to stop compromising with yourself.

That's what Kimberly did. The cancer just clarified how powerful it can be to make the decision to prioritize what's most important. As she shared, "It was permission to do what I wanted—not in a hedonistic way—permission to do what I felt was really right. Even if it went counter to convention and other people's expectations, even if it meant being a disappointment or not living up to other people's version of success. . . . What cancer did for me, it said: *You have permission, if you choose to decide.*"

Ten years after her diagnosis, Kimberly is cancer-free and still holding up her boundaries to that same high standard. The only difference is that she no longer needs the pink slips of paper to stand her ground and prioritize what matters. Her business continues to thrive, but Kimberly doesn't take late meetings, she doesn't compromise on being home for dinner, and she's created her own definition of success.

We never expect the detours, but sometimes the rerouting and the splintering of the path is an opportunity to see new potential. We're all given different seasons, but God and the universe conspire to help us—just not always in ways we recognize.

When things are difficult and we are looking for redemption or saving, sometimes it's not the situation that changes—it's us. We shift our perspective, our opinions, and our beliefs (many times in ourselves). Thank God for unanswered prayers because those are the moments where we are molded and shaped into the women we were truly designed to be.

Straying from the charted path is an opportunity to see new potential. But we have to be open to it, we have to be willing to understand that the purpose of the struggle isn't to change us but to help us become the best version of ourselves.

COMING FULL CIRCLE

I shifted and heard the thin white paper underneath me rip ever so slightly. Kate had just cried out, and I knew she was about to wake up hungry, so I pulled her close and swaddled the blanket tighter around her chubby newborn body. I heard the door behind me open, and I heard Dr. Elmquist give a happy sigh as she caught sight of me holding my beautiful girl.

"I haven't been in this room for over two years," I said, smiling as I glanced around. Even in all my numerous infertility and eventual maternity visits with her, I had surprisingly never stepped foot back in this room. "You probably don't remember . . ."

"I know," she told me gently. "I purposely never put you back in here, but I thought it might feel good for you today to see how far you've gone— and how much you've grown—over these past few years."

Lucky me to have a doctor who lives *On Purpose* and sees her work not as a deliverer of babies, but as a builder of women.

That period of my life was hard—and I would never want to relive it, but I also wouldn't trade it for anything. It's made me who I am today. And God knows how happy I am, that through that fight I ended up with Kate.

Getting derailed is sometimes just part of the path—it's the part you didn't plan for, it's the part you didn't know even existed, but it's imperative for you in becoming *you*.

What matters is that you choose to just keep moving forward.

LIES THAT HOLD US BACK:

- I'm always so unlucky.
- Nothing ever goes as I planned.
- With my goals, I seem to lose my motivation.
- I always make the same mistakes.

TRUTHS THAT MOVE US FORWARD:

- I embrace challenges because they make me stronger.
- When I get off track, it doesn't mean I've failed because it's a chance to make needed adjustments.
- When I make it a habit to check in on my goals, I feel motivated.
- Seeing mistakes as opportunities allows me to be open to new possibilities.

SPRINGBOARD: Creating a clear picture of your future vision is an important first step in reaching your dreams. Gather some magazines and create a vision board for what you want your life to look like for the next 12 months. Share with friends online to build in some accountability.

CONCLUSION

Choosing to Choose

You were designed for greatness.

There. I've said it. Take it in and let it sit for a minute. How does it feel? Like a thousand butterflies caught inside your stomach? Or does it feel like the humming of electricity coursing through your veins? Or maybe it feels like a granite stone resting cool and heavy on your chest?

No matter how that phrase feels inside, it's true. Every one of us has a purpose that was made to be bigger than ourselves—to bring satisfaction and joy to our lives and to the lives of others.

It's okay if this idea scares you a little bit. I'd be surprised if it didn't. But you got this far through this book because deep down you can feel it resonating in your soul.

THE UNIVERSAL TRUTH

You may question it and even ask yourself if this is the stuff of Harry Potter's universe. Is it just wishful thinking, as if you're hoping Hagrid will ride in on his motorcycle to tell you you're someone special? Is it a silly dream to think you are a part of something much bigger?

You were designed for

GREATNESS.

I wondered the same until astrophysicist (and scientific badass) Neil deGrasse Tyson shared irrefutable scientific evidence that quieted the rumbling doubts inside my head. It was the first time I truly understood my role in the universe, so I want to share this gift with you. He explained:

> The atoms of your body are traceable to stars that have exploded across the galaxy. Out of that scattered enrichment forms the next generations of star systems that have the ingredients that will make planets . . .
>
> Here we are on Earth: we wake up, eat breakfast, go to work, go to school, take care of the home—we are a participant in an ecosystem. And so, when you pull all this together, you realize it's not that we are here and the universe is there. It's not that we are humans and everything else isn't. It's that we are a participant in a great unfolding of cosmic events. And for me that gives us a sense of belonging.
>
> That's a cosmic perspective that allows you to sit up straight, look around, and say, "I belong to something bigger than my daily routine." It's a gift of twentieth century astrophysics to civilization that . . . you're not separate and distinct from the universe.
>
> You are part of the universe. You are in the universe. The universe is in you.

My atoms, your atoms, the atoms of the stars and the cosmos are all one and the same. You share the same DNA with the giant planet of Jupiter and the comets that zing through the galaxy at electrifying speeds. How can you *not* be made for greatness? You are made of stardust and supernovas.

When I understood that I belong to something bigger than my daily routine, it did encourage me to raise my chin higher, to pull my shoulders back, and it got me to question if I was squandering the gifts I have to offer. After all, I'm an important part of the universe . . . and so are you.

But here's the biggest catch of all—I know I've said that phrase before in this book, but there's no place it's truer than with this life-defining truth: life doesn't hand out participation awards. It's not an activity where we all get a gold star for simply showing up. Honestly, that kind of thing drives me crazy, where we celebrate mediocrity. Like when my kids' school hands out trophies and certificates to every student because they did the expected—they arrived at school every day.

It's not enough to just show up, to punch the clock and do the expected. You were made for more than checklists and carpool; you were made for more than expense reports or long, boring meetings where nothing gets accomplished.

Remember those big dreams you had when you were young? Don't choose to settle for less.

Living in mediocrity is stealing all your joy.

PLEASE DON'T FEED THE ANIMALS

It's okay if you feel like you've been struggling.
It's okay to admit you might not be fulfilled by the roles you currently play.
It's okay to want more, but it's up to you to go and get it.

If you really want to get that bigger life, you have to choose to take action—even when you don't want to. I understand if the idea of moving from where you are right now feels difficult. After all, it's where you're comfortable.

It reminds me of when I was a little girl and my mom would pull the still-warm sheets from the dryer. I would scurry onto the bed and flip over on my back as she billowed the covers, letting them float down and gently settle on top of me. I remember lying still and unmoving, feeling warm and comfortable . . . wishing I could stay there forever.

But we cannot live long under those sheets; we cannot pull the blankets over our heads. If we do, we will become complacent—the sheets will slowly grow cold and our bodies will begin to ache from inactivity.

Right now, you have a choice: feed the lies or feed the truth. You can only feed one, but whichever you choose will become your own reality.

When we make decisions based on our visions, that's when we lean heavily on our truth. We need to start making choices based on where we want to go—not where we are right now.

Having an *On Purpose* life gives you direction. It drives your decisions and helps you define how you want to act, where you want to focus, when you want to grow—and what you are living for.

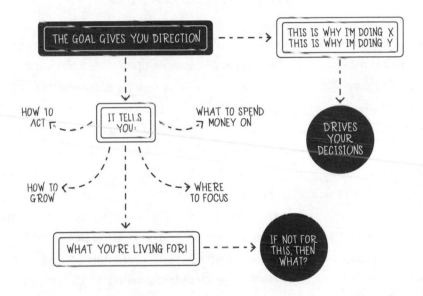

FEED YOUR LIES OR FEED YOUR TRUTH

YOU CAN FEED ONLY ONE

THE GOAL GIVES YOU DIRECTION

THIS IS WHY I'M DOING X
THIS IS WHY I'M DOING Y

HOW TO ACT

IT TELLS YOU:

WHAT TO SPEND MONEY ON

DRIVES YOUR DECISIONS

HOW TO GROW

WHERE TO FOCUS

WHAT YOU'RE LIVING FOR!

IF NOT FOR THIS, THEN WHAT?

Honestly, it's not a question of if you *can* do it . . . it's a question of whether you are willing to make the choice.

After all, if you can sit in the rain with your hands frozen to an umbrella while your kid plays soccer for two days straight, you, my friend, can do anything. You just have to decide that you can.

We were not born thinking *I can't*—thank goodness, because otherwise none of us would have figured out how to walk on these two sticks we call legs, and we definitely would have thrown in the towel the first time we skinned our knees when we took the training wheels off our bikes.

When you choose that you *can* and want to live differently, you will make it happen.

It's true, there will be days where it feels difficult to step outside of the circle of comfort you've always known. And yes, it will sometimes be hard to stand in your truth when others don't agree.

But it will be easy to find joy when you are living life true to yourself and your potential.

BUSTING FREE OF THE BOX

I had a conversation with God a few months ago—probably around the time I was writing chapter 6 of this book and gearing up for that next chapter on fear. At that point in my writing, I had already starting pulling deeply at the roots of who I had been—or at least the "who" I had been showing the world.

I knew I had to dig deeper still, and I realized I needed some help, so in my conversation with God, in my mind's eye, I handed Him a little box. It was simply made—just a few pieces of plain pinewood hammered roughly together with thick nails. I didn't need to explain the box to Him because He already knew exactly what it was: it was the tiny box I had been doing my damnedest to squeeze into for the past forty-some-odd years.

I prayerfully asked for help in smashing it. That's how I found myself on a Wednesday afternoon, with God beside me, swinging a hammer ferociously at that box in my mind. We didn't stop until the wood had torn free of the nails and the slats of lumber were jagged and battered beyond recognition. There was no way that box could ever be made whole again, which was exactly what I wanted.

I wanted to be free to step fully, wholly, authentically into the life that had been designed for me. I didn't want to give myself an opportunity to ever try and make myself small again. I was ready to take up more space, to step completely into a life *On Purpose*, where I didn't worry about what everyone else thinks or how they might judge. I was ready to live up to the promise made for me.

I had to make a decision. I had to decide that I will be in charge of my life—this a lifelong agreement with myself. I was tired of trading my life in exchange for the acceptance of others.

I think you are tired too. In fact, I know it. You are here reading this book at this very moment because you know it's time for more.

You are here because you are ready.

I'm ready too. Come find me and let's do this together.

UNLOCK YOUR OWN LIES AND TURN THEM INTO TRUTHS.

USING THE CAMERA ON YOUR SMART PHONE, SCAN THE CODE
ABOVE OR GO TO TANYADALTON.COM/ONPURPOSECLOSING

BONUS CONTENT

Back in chapter 6, I shared a way to invest in yourself by creating an Action Road Map. In that example, I shared how a young magical boy could eventually defeat an evil wizard. I chose that funny example because I wanted you to see how easy it can be to start gaining momentum. My deepest wish with this book is that it spurs you to take action in your own life, so I want to share a real-life example to help inspire you to create your own map.

Let's imagine your Cathedral is to grow your own company to eight figures, allowing you to start a foundation that helps promote leadership in young girls.* But right now you are sitting under the buzzing fluorescent lights in a tiny little cubicle toiling away for a large company. You know you are in the right industry, but the work you are doing isn't going to take you far.** You feel like you are in a rut, and that Cathedral seems so far away that you can barely see it.

---

* How much do you love that Cathedral? Me too!
** And, quite frankly, if your boss asks you to pick up bagels for the next meeting one more time, you might just lose it.

We'll start by wayfinding and creating your landmarks: You know that starting your own business is an important part of this path, so that seems possible in the next five years or so. When you look at what's practical, you decide that you probably need to get a higher level of experience at your current company in order to really have a nice launch pad for the business. You decide that you'll need to be promoted at work to the director level. To do that you need to get an advanced certification, create a portfolio of your work, and do a better job of networking within your company.

Your wayfinding map might look like this:

RIGHT NOW · GET ADVANCED CERTIFICATIONS · CREATE PORTFOLIO OF WORK · INCREASE NETWORKING · GET PROMOTED TO DIRECTOR LEVEL · START OWN CONSULTING COMPANY · GROW 8-FIGURE COMPANY & START A FOUNDATION

Next let's focus on how we'll take action by moving toward one of those Priority Landmarks. An advanced certification will definitely increase your chances of a promotion, so let's brainstorm the steps you need to take to reach that landmark.

You determine the steps you need to take are:

1. Research possible certifications
2. List application requirements for each
3. Gather all paperwork needed for applications
4. Fill out financial aid/loan paperwork
5. Apply for certification program
6. Create a study/focus time plan
7. Complete all certification work
8. Study for certification exam
9. Ace the test

As I mentioned back in chapter 6, we need to take a second to acknowledge that it's okay if you have no idea what all the steps might be—remember this is just a framework to help you start taking action. You can always adjust your Action Road Map as you learn more about the process. For now, just brainstorm what you think you need to do and write that down.

Then start grouping steps together. Look for ways that the different steps can be combined into one milestone. We can group based on time needed or dependency on one another.

In this case we might group our steps like this:

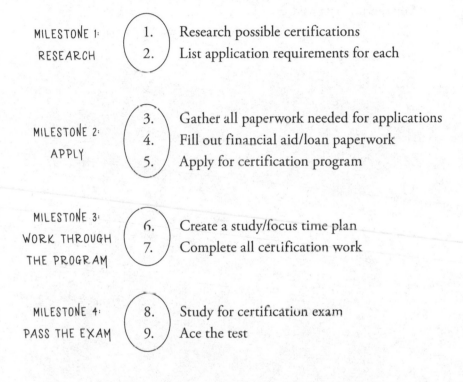

MILESTONE 1:
RESEARCH

1. Research possible certifications
2. List application requirements for each

MILESTONE 2:
APPLY

3. Gather all paperwork needed for applications
4. Fill out financial aid/loan paperwork
5. Apply for certification program

MILESTONE 3:
WORK THROUGH
THE PROGRAM

6. Create a study/focus time plan
7. Complete all certification work

MILESTONE 4:
PASS THE EXAM

8. Study for certification exam
9. Ace the test

Having these milestones is incredibly important in attaining your goals and ultimately in getting you to your Cathedral.

In our example, Milestone #1 (Research) could have a measurable outcome by deciding that you'll have a list of the top three programs you want to apply to with a deadline of two weeks. Milestone #2 (Apply) may have a deadline of one month. You'll know you've reached that milestone because you'll have all your applications completed and sent in. The key with milestones is making sure you have that outcome crystal clear—you want to know when you've accomplished each one!

The accountability you get from the Action Road Map is huge. And it helps you build momentum! When we started with this example, you were sitting in a job that felt like a dead end, unsure of how to proceed. Now where are you? Instead of being overwhelmed by these daunting goals, you have four milestones to work toward. It's completely achievable—and you plan to reach the first one in two weeks!

Momentum achieved.

ACKNOWLEDGMENTS

Writing the acknowledgments section of a book is one of the hardest parts of the entire writing process. You see, there are not nearly enough pages to express my gratitude for all the people who deserve recognition for all the work that goes into creating a book—from edits to design to marketing to the thousands of little things that support me and this message. I am grateful for every one of you. Know that if your name is not included in these pages, it's only because I don't have nearly enough room to truly express my gratitude.

John, a couple of lines in a book cannot do justice to who you are and what you mean to me. This book wouldn't be here without you. You are the one who believes in me every single time I don't believe in myself. You are the one who tells me I can when I wonder if I can't. And you are the one who loves me, even when I worry that I am unlovable. This life of ours is pretty incredible, and I am grateful to get to wake up each day next to you. Iloveyouso.

Jack, what a year it's been writing this book as I've watched you step into living your own life On Purpose. Watching you start to spread your wings as you step into adulthood is one of the greatest gifts I've been given.

Kate, I want to be you when I grow up. To be fourteen and to stand strong in who you are and what you believe makes me incredibly proud. I am continually amazed that I get to be your mom.

Mom and Dad, you were the first ones to teach me what purpose means. You taught me I could be anything I dreamed I could be—what a gift it is to grow up in a world with a healthy disregard for the impossible.

The Herridge Family, I wrote this book while we both felt we were in the trenches. I know you felt like those virtual happy hour dates saved you, but they saved me too. When it was time to dedicate this book, I knew it was for you. You have fiercely loved me and my family unconditionally. You are the other side of my soul.

To all of my friends and family—too countless to mention—I am so grateful for every note of encouragement, every text that came at just the right moment, each little bit helped push me up this hill. And for that I am grateful. I do want to quickly mention a few of you were absolutely instrumental in helping me get this book out into the world . . .

Emma Alexander, Heather Argus, and Siobhan Mountain, you have truly helped bring this book to life. You bring me to life. Thank you for reading every round of edits, for insanely beautiful graphics, and for giving this message a voice.

Brittney Lynn and Maggie Beaudouin, how can I possibly every express how much I love the two of you? Sometimes I think you know me better than I know myself. Your dedication and the work of the entire Human Connection Agency has helped me give my message a voice. You two are with me for the long haul.

This year of transformation and growth would not be complete without saying thank you to you, Ali Brown. You are so much more than a coach and mentor, you have reminded me of who I am and who I can become. I know without question God placed you on my path on purpose.

Emily Aarons, you opened my eyes to so much wonder in this world and within myself. Thank you for helping to see my gifts, and thank you for loving me so abundantly that it helped me love myself even more.

Steph Tuss, Myoshia Boykin-Anderson, Tracy Harrison, Brandi Bernoskie, Emily Countryman, Sara Yagoub, Abi Wangombe, Sarah Beth Aubrey, Michelle Bosch, Jereshia Hawk, Sunny Smith, Marshawn Evans-Daniels, Allie Casazza—knowing you were in my corner and that I could call on you at a moment's notice has made all the difference in the world to me. Thank you.

The women of The Trust who are my sisters in business. I truly wish every woman could know the value of surrounding herself with women like you. Women who lead, who encourage, who share abundantly and who continually push me to be my best.

My teams at Thomas Nelson and Yates & Yates—thanks for helping bring this book into the world. It's such an important message that I feel honored to carry, I am grateful you believe in this message as much as I do.

To the my extended family: the members of the Intentional CEO Mentorship, the podcast listeners, the *JOMO* readers, the women of my community, the brave women who allowed me to share their stories—I thought of you with every word I wrote. I sat down and pictured you as I sat typing away of my computer in the early mornings. Thank you for allowing my fire to burn brightly.

NOTES

This section includes a list of references, citations, and sources of inspiration. I've tried to be as thorough as I possibly can and have done my best to hunt down the original sources whenever possible. That said, I'm sure there may be a mistake or two somewhere in the book by attributing the idea to the wrong source or not giving credit where it's due. If you find an error, please do let me know and I'll make sure to make any corrections in future printings of the book. Thank you.

INTRODUCTION

xxvii "Take yawns, for example": Inspired by Malcolm Gladwell, *The Tipping Point: How Little Things Can Make a Big Difference* (Boston: Back Bay Books, 2013), 9.

CHAPTER 1: CHOOSE TO DISRUPT YOUR PATTERNS

4 "Did you know that": Michael Bergeisen, "The Neuroscience of Happiness," *Greater Good Magazine*, September 22, 2010, https://greatergood.berkeley.edu/article/item/the_neuroscience_of_happiness.

6 "Michael Pollan explained it": Michael Pollan, *How to Change Your Mind* (New York: Penguin Press, 2018), 15, 16.

10 "[Scientists] have determined": Harold S. Kushner, *When Bad Things Happen to Good People* (New York: Anchor Books, 2004), 72.

12 "Myoshia Boykin-Anderson has a past": Myoshia Boykin-Anderson, interview with author, May 20, 2020.

16 "Meaghan B Murphy is one of": Meaghan Murphy, "159: Living a Fully Charged Life with Meaghan Murphy," in *The Intentional Advantage Podcast*, produced by Tanya Dalton, 30:06, https://tanyadalton.com /podcasts/episode-159-living-a-fully-charged-life-with-meaghan-murphy.

16 "There must be a pony": Peter Robinson, *How Ronald Reagan Changed My Life* (New York: Regan Books, 2003), chap. 1, quoted in Tatiana Morales, "Writing for Ronald Reagan," CBS News, July 30, 2003, https://www.cbsnews.com/news/writing-for-ronald-reagan/.

18 "If you were like most kids": Po Bronson and Ashley Merryman, "The Creativity Crisis," *Newsweek*, July 10, 2010, https://www .newsweek.com/creativity-crisis-74665.

21 "In the predawn hours": Joe Sharkey, "Helping the Stars Take Back the Night," Business, *New York Times*, August 30, 2008, https://www.nytimes.com/2008/08/31/business/31essay.html.

CHAPTER 2: CHOOSE YOUR IDENTITY

24 "As I bent over the washboard": Henry Louis Gates Jr., "Madam Walker, the First Black American Woman to Be a Self-Made Millionaire," PBS, https://www.pbs.org/wnet/african-americans -many-rivers-to-cross/history/100-amazing-facts/madam-walker-the -first-black-american-woman-to-be-a-self-made-millionaire/.

24 "wanted to create this larger": "Hair Care Millionaire," in *Mysteries at the Museum*, hosted by Don Wildman, video, 03:42, Travel Channel, https://www.travelchannel.com/videos/hair-care-millionaire-0243883.

25 "one of the ways": Simon Sinek, *The Infinite Game* (New York: Portfolio, 2019), 141.

27 "Researchers were given access": Deborah D. Danner, David A. Snowdon, and Wallace V. Friesen, "Positive Emotions in Early Life and Longevity: Findings from the Nun Study," *Journal of Personality and Social Psychology* 80, no. 5 (2001): 804–13, https://www.apa.org /pubs/journals/releases/psp805804.pdf.

30 "For example, did you know": Vanessa M. Patrick and Henrik Hagtvedt, "'I Don't' Versus 'I Can't': When Empowered Refusal Motivates Goal-Directed Behavior," *Journal of Consumer Research* 39, no. 2 (August 2012): 371–81, https://academic.oup.com/jcr/article /39/2/371/1797950.

31 "Here's an upsetting fact": Soo Youn, "Women Are Less Aggressive Than Men When Applying for Jobs, Despite Getting Hired More Frequently: LinkedIn," ABC News, March 7, 2019, https://abcnews .go.com/Business/women-aggressive-men-applying-jobs-hired -frequently-linkedin/story?id=61531741.

31 "It's an anecdote": Susan Chira, "Why Women Aren't C.E.O.s: According to Women Who Almost Were," News Analysis, *New York Times*, July 21, 2017, https://www.nytimes.com/2017/07/21/sunday -review/women-ceos-glass-ceiling.html.

31 "The article noted": Chira, "Why Women Aren't C.E.O.s."

32 "As former CEO of DuPont": Chira, "Why Women Aren't C.E.O.s."

32 "According to Hannah Riley Bowles": Stephanie Thomson, "A Lack of Confidence Isn't What's Holding Back Working Women," *The Atlantic*, September 20, 2018, https://www.theatlantic.com/family /archive/2018/09/women-workplace-confidence-gap/570772/.

32 "This is why girls tend": Tara Sophia Mohr, "Why Women Don't Apply for Jobs Unless They're 100% Qualified," *Harvard Business Review*, August 25, 2014, https://hbr.org/2014/08/why-women-dont -apply-for-jobs-unless-theyre-100-qualified.

35 "Why would anyone": Birender Ahluwalia, "Feel Like a Fraud? You Might Be Suffering From the Imposter Syndrome," DNA, May 29, 2016, https://www.dnaindia.com/lifestyle/column-if-you-feel-like -and-imposter-you-need-to-read-this-2217913.

37 "I really do think he believed": "194: Using Your Past to Strengthen Your Future with Mary Marantz," in *The Intentional Advantage Podcast*, produced by Tanya Dalton, 31:58, https://tanyadalton.com /podcasts/episode-194-using-your-past-to-strengthen-your-future -with-mary-marantz.

CHAPTER 3: CHOOSE TO SEE YOUR FUTURE

48 "require the same foundation": Rick Antonson, "What Is Cathedral Thinking?," *Cathedral Thinking* (blog), https://cathedralthinking.com/.

50 "UCLA psychologist Hal Hershfield": Hal Ersner-Hershfield, G. Elliott Wimmer, and Brian Knutson, "Saving for the Future Self: Neural Measures of Future Self-Continuity Predict Temporal Discounting," *Social Cognitive and Affective Neuroscience* 4, no. 1 (March 2009): 85–92, https://academic.oup.com/scan/article/4/1/85/1613040.

51 "In the present, you're": Melissa Dahl, "It's Time to Get Acquainted with Your Future Self," *The Cut*, January 14, 2015, https://www.thecut.com/2015/01/time-to-get-acquainted-with-future-you.html.

54 "ignite the passion": Amy Bridges, "145: Defining Your North Star: How Your Past Can Lead to Your Future," in *The Intentional Advantage Podcast*, produced by Tanya Dalton, 26:33, https://tanyadalton.com/podcasts/episode-145-defining-your-north-star-how-your-past-can-lead-to-your-future.

56 "adapting well in the face": David Palmiter et al., "Building Your Resilience," American Psychological Association, 2012, https://www.apa.org/topics/resilience.

56 "Did you know that": Liz Fosslien and Mollie West Duffy, "This Is How Envy, Anger and Regret Affect Your Decisions at Work," *Fast Company*, April 30, 2019, https://www.fastcompany.com/90340327/this-is-how-envy-anger-and-regret-affect-our-decisions-at-work.

59 "We went from negative": Amy Lacey, interview with author, September 8, 2020.

59 "Why would anyone write": *Everything Is Copy—Nora Ephron: Scripted and Unscripted*, written and directed by Jacob Bernstein, (New York: HBO Documentary Films, 2016), https://www.hbo.com/documentaries/everything-is-copy.

CHAPTER 4: CHOOSE TO FIND YOUR FOCUS

64 "I felt like I was holding": Amy Jo Martin, "140: Why Not Now with Amy Jo Martin," in *The Intentional Advantage Podcast*,

produced by Tanya Dalton, 25:54, https://tanyadalton.com/podcasts /episode-140-why-not-now-with-amy-jo-martin.

70 "Agatha Christie was a terrible speller": Linda S. Siegel, "Agatha Christie's Learning Disability," *Canadian Psychology* 29, no. 2 (April 1988): 213–16, https://www.researchgate.net/publication/232441698 _Agatha_Christie's_learning_disability.

71 "Shakira, who is one": Jacob Shamsian and Chelsea Pineda, "Shakira's Teacher Told Her She Had a Bad Voice and Banned Her from the School Choir," Business Insider, March 18, 2016, https://www .businessinsider.com/shakira-banned-from-school-choir-2016-3.

75 "Aviation management expert Julian": Jessica Hullinger, "12 Ways Airports Are Secretly Manipulating You," Mental Floss, July 22, 2017, https://www.mentalfloss.com/article/64808/12-behind-scenes-secrets -airports.

76 "In fact, 14 percent": Juan Marcos González et al., "Trading Health Risks for Glory: A Reformulation of the Goldman Dilemma," *Sports Medicine* 48, no. 8 (August 2018): 1963–69, https://pubmed.ncbi .nlm.nih.gov/29498027/.

77 "Brooke Harrington, a professor": Joe Pinsker, "The Reason Many Ultrarich People Aren't Satisfied with Their Wealth," *The Atlantic*, December 4, 2018, https://www.theatlantic.com/family/archive /2018/12/rich-people-happy-money/577231/.

78 "When you're in those deep trenches": Kristen Ley, interview with author, podcast episode 164: "Making Big Shifts in Business and Beyond" in *The Intentional Advantage Podcast*, produced by Tanya Dalton, 33:00, https://tanyadalton.com/podcasts/episode-164-making -big-shifts-in-business-beyond-with-kristen-ley.

CHAPTER 5: CHOOSE TO MAKE A PLAN

84 "Here's a fascinating fact": Jan Souman and Susanne Diederich, "Walking in Circles," Max-Planck-Gesellschaft, August 20, 2009, https://www.mpg.de/596269/pressRelease200908171.

89 "In fact, 81 percent of people": J. C. Norcross and D. J. Vangarelli,

"The Resolution Solution: Longitudinal Examination of New Year's Change Attempts," *Journal of Substance Abuse Treatment* 1, no. 2 (1988–89): 127–34, https://pubmed.ncbi.nlm.nih.gov/2980864/.

96 "In fact, one Yale University study": Amy Wrzesniewski and Jane E. Dutton, "Crafting a Job: Revisioning Employees as Active Crafters of Their Work," *Academy of Management Review* 26, no. 2 (April 2001): 179–201, https://spinup-000d1a-wp-offload-media. s3.amazonaws.com/faculty/wp-content/uploads/sites/6/2019/06 /Craftingajob_Revisioningemployees_000.pdf.

96 "In the study, the custodians": David Zax, "Want to Be Happier at Work? Learn How from These 'Job Crafters,'" *Fast Company*, June 3, 2012, https://www.fastcompany.com/3011081/want-to-be-happier-at -work-learn-how-from-these-job-crafters.

97 "One of my favorite studies": Jennifer Paley, "Praising Intelligence: Costs to Children's Self-Esteem and Motivation," Stanford: Bing Nursery School, October 1, 2011, https://bingschool.stanford.edu /news/praising-intelligence-costs-childrens-self-esteem-and-motivation.

97 "We've all heard": John Greathouse, "5 Time-Tested Success Tips from Amazon Founder Jeff Bezos," *Forbes*, April 30, 2013, https ://www.forbes.com/sites/johngreathouse/2013/04/30/5-time-tested -success-tips-from-amazon-founder-jeff-bezos/.

99 "When psychologists dove deeper": T. Gilovich and V. H. Medvec, "The Temporal Pattern to the Experience of Regret," *Journal of Personality and Social Psychology* 67, no. 3 (1994): 357–65, https ://psycnet.apa.org/record/1995-05382-001.

CHAPTER 6: CHOOSE TO INVEST IN YOURSELF

107 "Our brain is wired"; Kent C. Berridge and Terry E. Robinson, "What Is the Role of Dopamine in Reward: Hedonic Impact, Reward Learning, or Incentive Salience?," *Brain Research Reviews* 28, no. 3 (1998): 309–69, https://www.sciencedirect.com/science/article /abs/pii/S0165017398000198?via%3Dihub.

112 "She replied, 'You didn't ruin'": Marshawn Evans Daniels, *Believe*

Bigger: Discover the Path to Your Life Purpose (New York: Howard Books, 2018), 27.

113 "Marshawn told me, 'You'"; Marshawn Evans Daniels, "061: Investing in Yourself with Marshawn Evans Daniels," in *The Intentional Advantage Podcast*, produced by Tanya Dalton, 30:39, https:// tanyadalton.com/podcasts/episodes-061-investing-in-yourself-with -marshawn-evans-daniels.

114 "There is no bad side": M. S. Hagger et al., "A Multilab Preregistered Replication of the Ego-Depletion Effect," *Perspectives on Psychological Science* 11, no. 4 (July 2016): 546–73, https://journals.sagepub.com /doi/full/10.1177/1745691616652873.

114 "We now know that": Office of Communications, "Study: Brain Battles Itself Over Short-Term Rewards, Long-Term Goals," Princeton University, October 14, 2004, https://pr.princeton.edu/news/04 /q4/1014-brain.htm.

116 "Jessica, who chased down": Jessica Honegger, interview with author, November 13, 2020.

116 "According to the Mayo Clinic": Micah Dorfner, "How to Overcome the Top 5 Fitness Barriers," Mayo Clinic, July 27, 2015, https:// newsnetwork.mayoclinic.org/discussion/how-to-overcome-the-top-5 -fitness-barriers/.

118 "I definitely was one": Dorothy Beal, "110: Dorothy Beal on the Power of Self Love," in *The Intentional Advantage Podcast*, produced by Tanya Dalton, 30:50, https://tanyadalton.com/podcasts/episode -110-dorothy-beal-on-the-power-of-self-love.

121 "When you start out": Neil Gaiman, keynote address, University of the Arts, 134th Commencement, May 17, 2012, Philadelphia, transcript and video, 19:55, https://www.uarts.edu/neil-gaiman -keynote-address-2012.

122 "I'm gonna tell you what": Lynn Hirschberg, "Greta Gerwig Can't Help Sounding Like an Old Man When She Talks About the Internet," *W*, March 21, 2017, https://www.wmagazine.com/story /greta-gerwig-directing-debut-lady-bird-interview/.

124 "This phenomenon is called": A. Bruk, S. G. Scholl, and H. Bless, "Beautiful Mess Effect: Self-Other Differences in Evaluation of Showing Vulnerability," *Journal of Personality and Social Psychology* 115, no. 2 (2018): 192–205, https://psycnet.apa.org/record/2018 -34832-002.

CHAPTER 7: CHOOSE TO RELEASE YOUR FEARS

130 "The number-one fear": Christopher Ingraham, "America's Top Fears: Public Speaking, Heights and Bugs," *Washington Post*, October 30, 2014, https://www.washingtonpost.com/news/wonk /wp/2014/10/30/clowns-are-twice-as-scary-to-democrats-as-they-are -to-republicans/.

130 "The odds of dying": "Odds of Dying," Injury Facts, https://injuryfacts .nsc.org/all-injuries/preventable-death-overview/odds-of-dying/?.

140 "Do whatever it takes": Neil deGrasse Tyson, "The Scientific Method," in *Neil deGrasse Tyson Teaches Scientific Thinking and Communication*, MasterClass, video, 14:13, https://www.masterclass .com/classes/neil-degrasse-tyson-teaches-scientific-thinking-and -communication/chapters/the-scientific-method.

144 "A Harvard Business School study": Allison Wood Brooks, "Get Excited: Reappraising Pre-Performance Anxiety as Excitement," *Journal of Experimental Psychology* 143, no. 3 (2014): 1144–58, https://www.apa.org/pubs/journals/releases/xge-a0035325.pdf.

CHAPTER 8: CHOOSE TO CREATE THE TIME

150 "I read Dr. Gay Hendrick's description": Gay Hendricks, *The Big Leap: Conquer Your Hidden Fear and Take Life to the Next Level* (New York: HarperCollins, 2009), 180–81.

156 "Your quality of work": Tom Rath, *Eat, Move, Sleep: How Small Choices Lead to Big Changes* (Arlington, VA: Missionday, 2013).

157 "thin . . . like butter that": J. R. R. Tolkien, *The Lord of the Rings* (1954; repr., New York: Houghton Mifflin Company, 2004), 32.

158 "As she put it,": Donna Sava, "146: How Boundaries Will Set You

Free," in *The Intentional Advantage Podcast*, produced by Tanya Dalton, 24:26, https://tanyadalton.com/podcasts/episode-146-how -boundaries-will-set-you-free.

159 "Play is essential": Robert Murray and Catherine Ramstetter, "The Crucial Role of Recess in School," *Pediatrics* 131, no. 1 (January 2013): 183–88, https://pediatrics.aappublications.org/content/131/1/183.

160 "Tyanna told me she": Tyanna Smith, "148: Waiting to Start Our Dreams," in *The Intentional Advantage Podcast*, produced by Tanya Dalton, 26:08, https://tanyadalton.com/podcasts/episode-148-waiting -to-start-our-dreams.

161 "Too often we confuse": Wooden's original quote: "Never mistake activity for achievement." John Wooden, "Motivational Quotes," The Wooden Effect, https://www.thewoodeneffect.com/motivational-quotes/.

162 "Every day we have": Anne Craig, "Discovery of 'Thought Worms' Opens Window to the Mind," *Queen's Gazette*, July 13, 2020, https ://www.queensu.ca/gazette/stories/discovery-thought-worms-opens -window-mind.

163 "Dana expressed this": Tanya Dalton, liveWELL Method, live call, April 2020, https://learn.inkwellpress.com/p/livewell-method2.

164 "Jenny Johnson shared her big": Tanya Dalton, The Intentional CEO, laser coaching, August 2020, https://tanyadalton.com/ceo-backup.

CHAPTER 9: CHOOSE TO GIVE GRACE

178 "On one of our live": Tanya Dalton, liveWELL Method, live call, August 18, 2020.

180 "Before/After [Existing Habit]": James Clear, *Atomic Habits: An Easy & Proven Way to Build Good Habits & Break Bad Ones* (New York: Penguin Random House, 2018), 110.

184 "Taska Sanford is a woman": Taska Sanford, "155: The Art of Knowing Where to Focus," in *The Intentional Advantage Podcast*, produced by Tanya Dalton, 25:06, https://tanyadalton.com/podcasts/episode-155 -the-art-of-knowing-where-to-focus.

184 "Breast cancer is one": Kimberly Gerber, interview by author, June 23, 2020.

CONCLUSION

193 "The atoms of your body": Neil deGrasse Tyson, "What You Know Is Not as Important as How You Think," in *Neil deGrasse Tyson Teaches Scientific Thinking and Communication*, MasterClass, video, 06:02, https://www.masterclass.com/classes/neil-degrasse-tyson -teaches-scientific-thinking-and-communication/chapters/what-you -know-is-not-as-important-as-how-you-think/.

ABOUT THE AUTHOR

TANYA DALTON is a wife, mother, entrepreneur, and recovering perfectionist. She is the CEO and founder of inkWELL Press Productivity Co., a seven-figure company focused on helping women confidently step into intentional leadership. Whether listening to Tanya's podcast, *The Intentional Advantage*, hearing her speak or visiting her social media feed, you'll walk away with real, actionable advice on living your best life at home and at work.

She is also a featured expert on several networks including NBC and Fox and is a VIP contributor for Entrepreneur.com. Tanya has been featured in some of the world's leading publications including *Forbes*, *Inc.*, Fast Company, and Real Simple.

Those who know her best describe Tanya as a mom who loves her family fiercely, isn't afraid to make a fool of herself, and wants nothing more than for you to stop overthinking and start living the life you really want.

TanyaDalton.com

Book Tanya for Your Next Speaking Event

TANYADALTON.COM/SPEAKING

FAST TRACK TO FREEDOM
Formula

FOR SERIOUS BUSINESS OWNERS WHO KNOW THERE'S MORE TO LIFE THAN BUSINESS.

The Fast Track to Freedom Formula will give you the tools, systems, and support to grow your business to seven figures without sacrificing your personal life. You can have the time, wealth, and lifestyle freedom you want and deserve.

Work with me and my team and learn how to run a successful, profitable, and productive business while working less so you can have thriving relationships and a rich personal life.

Go to TANYADALTON.COM/FTF to sign up!

TIME, WEALTH, AND LIFESTYLE FREEDOM

Goal Setting Planner

READY TO START LIVING A LIFE *ON PURPOSE*?

Tanya's goal setting planner is designed to help you take action using the four step process covered in this book: Reflection, Projection, Action, and Alteration. This is the only planner on the market where you'll find the IMPACT goal system shared in chapter 5, the Action Road Map™ from chapter 6, and the Goal Setting Matrix™ covered in chapter 8.

With monthly check-ins to help keep you on track and spots to make alterations and adjustments as you move through the year, this planner was created to help you start living the life you were designed for.

Available exclusively through inkWELL Press

INKWELLPRESS.COM/GOAL

INKWELL PRESS.
PRODUCTIVITY CO.